THE SOCIOLOGY
OF MANAGEMENT

For Christopher

THE SOCIOLOGY OF MANAGEMENT

M.I. Reed

*Lecturer, Department of Behaviour in Organisations,
University of Lancaster*

HARVESTER WHEATSHEAF

New York   London   Toronto   Sydney   Tokyo

First published 1989 by
Harvester Wheatsheaf
400 Campus, Maylands Avenue, Hemel Hempstead
Hertfordshire, HP2 7EZ
A division of
Simon & Schuster International Group

© Michael Reed 1989

Printed in Great Britain by
Antony Rowe Ltd, Chippenham, Wiltshire

British Library Cataloguing in Publication Data

Reed, Michael, *1950–*
The sociology of management
1. Business enterprise, Manpower.
Management. Sociological perspectives
I. Title
302.3'5

ISBN 0-7450-0387-7

3 4 5   93

CONTENTS

INTRODUCTION

The purpose of this book is to provide an assessment of the contribution that sociology has made to our understanding of the location and role of management within industrial capitalist societies.

The significance of management for an understanding of the dynamics of institutional change within modern society has been clearly recognised by sociologists since they first began to make sense of the long-term impact of industrial and political revolution occurring at the end of the eighteenth century. The increasing dominance of large-scale bureaucratic organisations from the latter half of the nineteenth century onwards was seen to signify a dramatic shift towards a qualitatively different form of institutional order in which managers (in the broadest sense of that term) emerged as one of the most strategically located interest groups. Not only were they portrayed as the major agents of industrial modernisation, but they were also seen as the prime beneficiaries of this process insofar as it initiated a redistribution of economic, political and social power that worked in their favour. Thus, Wolin[1] argues that one of the overarching themes of late nineteenth and early twentieth century social theory was the emergence of a new social order based on scientific principles and rational techniques formulated and applied by an élite of managers and administrators. This technocratic vision promised that scientific method and managerial expertise would greatly extend man's power over nature and society.

The unintended consequence of this movement in social thought and analysis was the sublimation, if not explicit assimilation, of moral and political problems within an engineering ideology that reduced the latter to the status of technical issues concerned with means rather than ends. Managers became the social and organisational engineers who designed and constructed the machinery through which this process could be enacted – that is, the process whereby moral and political problems were transformed into matters of technique.

This sociological interest in the managerial revolution has continued well into the twentieth century. It reached its apogee in that body of research and writing that predicted a divorce between ownership and control and the rise of a powerful and independent body of corporate technocrats as the most important structural transformation taking place in converging industrialised societies.[2] In this respect, managers and technocrats were seen as the midwives of a form of pluralistic industrialism that would spread out from the confines of western industrialised societies and eventually span the globe:

> The managers of enterprises, public and private, and their technical and professional associates are part of every industrializing elite. They are crucial to the success of any industrialization effort. Their policies and practices have far-flung influence in shaping the labour problems which emerge in industrializing societies. The role of management of enterprises, in contrast to earlier periods, now generally enjoys prestige in the economically developed countries.[3]

Yet, this continuing sociological interest in the managerial revolution has failed to produce a coherent and convincing account of the position and function of management within modern society. Research was spread across a wide range of topics, pursued through a bewildering diversity of theoretical perspectives encouraging intellectual fragmentation, and developed at a number of distinct and often isolated levels of analysis. A concern with the vital contribution management makes to institutional transformation was evident in many of the most important sociological works published after World War II.[4] This concern, however, usually remained implicit rather than explicit in that it was developed along with a large number of general themes in which it became gradually submerged and obscured. This book is intended to contribute to the process whereby a more focused sociological understanding of the nature of modern management may be developed.

The analysis that this book provides focuses upon a number of substantive themes that have directed sociological research on management such as control, conflict, work, class and change. Discussion of these themes is located within a conceptual framework that attempts to integrate three levels of analysis evident in sociological research on management. First, that research which approaches management as a sectional interest group that competes with other interest groups for scarce organisational resources. Second, that view which treats management as a general organisational process or resource and system of authority concerned with the structuring of work behaviour and relations within productive units. Third, that body of writing which focuses upon the class location and function of management within the stratification systems characteristic of advanced capitalist societies.

It is suggested that each of these levels of analysis can be accommodated within a conception of management as a social practice – that is, as a set of interrelated activities and mechanisms for assembling and regulating productive activity within work. This view of management, it will be argued, can facilitate a better understanding of the processes and structures through which power is mobilised and control achieved.

The earlier chapters are concerned with issues that are located at the group and organisational levels. Later chapters concentrate upon macro-level developments and their implications for the position and role of managers in industrial capitalist societies. For the most part, the analysis provided here relies on source material taken from either a North American or British context; limited empirical material taken from other societies is included, particularly in the latter stages of the discussion.

REFERENCES

1. Wolin, S., *Politics and Vision* (Allen & Unwin, London, 1961).
2. This issue is discussed at some length in Chapter five of this book.
3. Kerr, C., Dunlop, J.T., Harbison, F.H. and Myers, C.A., *Industrialism and Industrial Man* (Heinemann, London, 1960), p. 133. The various sociological theories that have been developed in an attempt to explain

the process of industrialisation and its long-term impact are reviewed in Kumar, K., *Prophecy and Progress: The Sociology of Industrial and Post-Industrial Society* (Allen Lane, London, 1978) and Leggatt, T., *The Evolution of Industrial Systems* (Croom Helm, London, 1985).
4. For example: Burnham, J., *The Managerial Revolution* (Penguin, Harmondsworth, 1945); Dahrendorf, R., *Class and Class Conflict in Industrial Society* (Routledge and Kegan Paul, London, 1959); Kerr, *et al.*, op. cit., (1960); Galbraith, J.K., *The New Industrial State* (Hamish Hamilton, London, 1967).

1

THEORETICAL
PERSPECTIVES

INTRODUCTION

The claim that we lack a systematic sociological understanding of management in the 'advanced societies'[1] has crystallised into a conventional orthodoxy that is deemed to require some sort of corrective response on the part of the sociological community.[2] Unfortunately, many of the responses that have been forthcoming unintentionally reinforce the confusion they are meant to dispel. This is true to the extent that they perpetuate the analytical fragmentation and methodological polarisation that has characterised the study of management as one of the most strategic social processes and institutions within our society.[3]

This opening chapter explores the various analytical perspectives and related methodologies that have been developed to study management, and outlines an alternative perspective that attempts to correct the deficiencies which this exploration reveals.[4] Its aim is to provide an integrated conceptual framework that will inform the discussion that follows in later chapters of managerial processes and structures in their encompassing institutional milieux. It also serves to identify the central substantive themes around which the latter discussion will be undertaken.

Each of the analytical perspectives reviewed and developed in this chapter focuses on management as an organisational mechanism and/or process geared to the co-ordination and control of productive activity. The need to link this organisationally focused level of analysis to wider institutional configurations of occupational structure and social class is highlighted in this chapter, but postponed as a major analytical and substantive issue to be returned to in Chapter Five.

THEORETICAL PERSPECTIVES ON MANAGEMENT

We can identify three major analytical perspectives that have shaped sociological research and analysis of management since the earlier decades of this century. These are the technical perspective, the political perspective and the critical perspective. Each of these has waxed and waned in intellectual popularity as the broader social context in which they have been developed has resonated with the cultural values and ideological appeals they entail.

These perspectives are important to the extent that they fulfil three crucial intellectual functions for those engaged in sociological research on management. First, they provide a characterisation of subject matter that establishes a focus for analysis. Second, they entail preferred models of explanation to account for the phenomena itemised and described under the previous characterisation. Third, they legitimate certain practical interventions in the course of social life in the furtherance of collective projects and deny that aura of legitimacy to competing intervention strategies. In short, they provide the analytical tools and ideological resources necessary to attain a minimally acceptable degree of intellectual coherence and operational viability.

Each of the perspectives mentioned above will be examined in the light of these three crucial intellectual functions. Initially, a general specification of each perspective will be outlined and this will be followed by a brief exposition of the work of individual researchers who are deemed to be representative of a particular perspective.

THE TECHNICAL PERSPECTIVE

The technical perspective offers a conception of management as a rationally designed and operationalised tool for the realisation of predominantly instrumental values concerned with the systematic co-ordination of social action on a massive scale and the long-term continuity this provides. Management is about means rather than ends; it constitutes the neutral social technology necessary to attain collective goals that are unrealisable without it. This conception of management as a formalised structure of rationally designed control systems geared to the attainment of technical effectiveness in human co-ordination is based on the assumption that organisations are the functionally indispensable mechanisms that institutionalise individual values and objectives into superhuman collectivities that outlive their creators. Formal organisations guarantee the social immortality of mortal individual human beings to the extent that they facilitate long-term institutional identity, continuity and stability in an uncertain and unforgiving world. Management is characterised as the organisational machinery that both enables and protects that sense of immortality in a social world where the conflict between sectional interests and the confusion it creates is endemic.

In this respect, the technical perspective raises that configuration of formal structural elements through which management takes on a clear conceptual identity and wider social purpose to reach the status of paramount theoretical and practical significance. These structural elements may be shaped into different forms along various dimensions, such as the extent of internal functional differentiation, the degree of centralised decision-making or the extensiveness of written rules and procedures. Yet the fact of empirical variation does not detract from the significance of this configuration of structural components as constituting the irreducible analytical core that provides the study of management with the minimally required degree of theoretical coherence and practical import. Without structure, the conception of management as an instrument of rational co-ordination and control loses all its theoretical power and technical utility. Explanations as to the conditions under which certain organisational types will prevail rather than others, and be more effective for task performance than alternative forms, are reduced to the status of low-level descriptive exercises bereft of that generalising capability necessary to sustain the most restricted type of prediction and control unless they are grounded in this structural model.

Given this concentrated analytical focus on the structural nature of management, the technical perspective relies on a systems approach to the study of organisations. A means-oriented conception of management, which concentrates on the structural mechanisms that ensure order and secure effective co-ordination and control over social interaction, encourages the formulation of an explanatory framework that treats organisations as social units that must fulfil certain functional needs or imperatives imposed on them by their environment. The manner in which these functional imperatives are identified and classified may vary to some degree between individual exponents of the systems approach.[5] However, the latter remain committed to an explanatory logic that accounts for the existence and persistence of management structures in terms of the contribution they make to the survival of the organisational system as a whole.

Change within the system is seen to result from the failure of the internal management structure to adapt to developments in the organisation's environment. Consequently, there is an imbalance, or disequilibrium, between the component parts of the structure, and this induces strain or tension within the system as a result of the inadequate performance of these components. Thus the pragmatic impulse behind the application of the systems approach in organisational analysis is to pinpoint those areas in which disequilibrium and consequent strain is occurring (due to faults in structural design) and help individual managers to take corrective action to restore an appropriate relationship between internal designs and external conditions.

In this sense, the overriding policy strategy or mission guiding the development of the technical perspective is the desire to enhance the effectiveness of structural design by ensuring that the dysfunctional consequences of organisational maladjustment are diagnosed and remedied as quickly as possible. This requires a detailed analysis of the demands various environmental contingencies – such as size, technological change, product differentiation, market specifications and informational needs – place upon the organisation and the extent to which these are met by established modes of internal co-ordination and control that have been adopted to fulfil these demands. The real test of an appropriate or adequate organisational design is the quality of functional fit between the internal structures through which management exercise control over the myriad of social transactions that take place within their organisation and the changing pattern of external environmental demands they are meant to meet.

The technical perspective has been the dominant intellectual construction through which the sociological analysis of management has been undertaken. It has come under increasing pressure, however, in more recent years as interest in the complex social processes that shape, if not direct, the dynamics of organisational change has developed. Undoubtedly, the focus on structure as a formal mechanism for co-ordinating and controlling task performance on a rational and continuous basis owes much to the intellectual inheritance bequeathed by the 'classical or traditional theory of organisations'.[6] The latter aspired to provide a general theory of management that was universal in its empirical scope and followed the logical system of deductive law-like explanation assumed to prevail in the natural sciences.[7] The realisation of a general theory of management was to be achieved through the formulation and reformulation of a continuing series of more refined conceptual frameworks through which the critical aspects of organisational structure could be identified. It was envisaged that increased conceptual refinement would also facilitate practical recommendations about the form of organisational structure that would be most appropriate regardless of situational or contextual variation.[8]

The universalistic aspirations of classical management theory have been severely criticised and rejected by contemporary researchers operating within the technical perspective.[9] Its lack of attention to empirical detail and the implications of contextual variation for structural redesign by management have also been roundly criticised.[10] Yet we should not underestimate the intellectual influence of the classical approach on modern systems approaches to management. The work of researchers such as Etzioni,[11] Thompson,[12] Lawrence and Lorsch,[13] and Pugh and Hickson[14] bears a close resemblance to the classical approach in a number of respects. First, organisational structure is treated as being conceptually synonymous with formal organisation. Second, explanations of how these structures exist and persist are framed in terms of a deterministic logic that assumes that institutionalised patterns of social relations impose themselves on organisational actors – including managers – in such a way that organisational development proceeds along a predetermined trajectory irrespective of human volition and action. Organisational change takes place behind the backs of organisational members, who remain in a condition of relative ignorance as to the internal dynamics of the former and its source in external circumstances that are beyond the determination of organisational designers. Third, managers can exercise some limited control over the pace and direction of structural redesign even though they are merely responding to, and attempting to cope with, a logic of structural development that operates in an autonomous manner.[15]

Increasing dissatisfaction with the deterministic predilections of those who advocated the adoption of a technical perspective in the analysis of management has led to the formulation of an alternative perspective that is grounded in a model of management as a political process in which power conflicts and their temporary resolution become central to an understanding of organisational change.

THE POLITICAL PERSPECTIVE

The political perspective promotes a view of management as a social process geared to the regulation of interest group conflict in an environment characterised by considerable uncertainty over the criteria through which effective organisational performance is assessed. As such, it signifies a clear break with the rationalism associated with the technical perspective. It reconceptualises management as consisting of a plurality of competing groups or coalitions that often come into conflict over decisions concerning the choice of organisational designs and temporarily resolve this disagreement through the exercise of power in one form or another. In direct contrast to the deterministic bias implicit in the technical perspective, political analyses of managerial decision-making over organisational design concentrate on the continually shifting balance of interests and power within management (particularly top management or the 'dominant coalition')[16] and its impact on the way in which the agenda for decision-taking is constructed.

The shift of focus from structure to process is not accidental; it exemplifies a rejection of the static and mechanistic conception of management that is deemed to inform the work of those operating within the technical perspective. The political perspective offers an approach that deals with individual managers as knowledgeable human agents functioning within a dynamic situation where both organisational means and outcomes can be substantially shaped by them. The main research effort of those advocating a political perspective on management has centred on the need to trace the sources of power available to various managerial coalitions, the degree of political skill with which the potential leverage they offer is utilised, and the extent to which the strategic mobilisation of power resources facilitates manipulative control over the frame of reference within which managerial decision-making occurs. Usually, researchers operating within this approach rely upon a power-dependence model of managerial power relations in which the capacity of a particular coalition to determine the agenda of decision-making (that is, its power) is seen to be a function of its ability to minimise dependence on others within the contingent constraints presented by the particular situation in which it is operating. Thus a complex combination of situationally determined opportunities and the level of political skill exhibited in utilising the potential for control which they offer to attain preferred decisional outcomes is seen to constitute a central focus for research endeavour by advocates of the political perspective.

The primary effect of the increasing popularity of the political perspective in the sociology of management has been expressed in the substantial rethink it has initiated about the assumptions underlying the orthodox model of management as a set of rationally designed and operationalised control systems effectively ensuring the realisation of instrumental objectives. This model has been subverted by a much more explicit recognition of management organisation as a political system in which institutional order and operating practices have to be continually reworked through the negotiated transactions between coalitions covering the total range of organisational personnel. While the exact nature and scope of this negotiating process is still the subject of debate, the 'pervasive pluralism'[17] of management organisation is a crucial point of theoretical reference for those who advocate a political perspective and stands in sharp contrast to the emphasis on formal regularity and consistency discovered within the technical approach.

Exponents of a political approach to the study of management have drawn extensively on an action frame of reference in organisational analysis.[18] The latter approaches organisational structures as continually reworked networks of social interaction in which the more stable features of formal control systems – hierarchy, rules, procedures, regulatory codes, monitoring techniques, etc. – are seen to constitute a background context that is subject to renegotiation through the routine transactions engaged in by all personnel. As a result, structure is redefined as a temporary patterning of the ebb and flow of interactional processes open to periodic reappraisal and reconstruction through negotiated agreements between participants. It loses its theoretical status as the primary factor determining social interaction and is conceptually transformed from a neutral instrument of social control into 'an emergent product of processes of negotiation and interpretation enacted by differentially placed participants within the jurisdiction of organisational rules and administrative programmes'.[19]

This reinforces the importance – both theoretical and practical – attached to the manner in which the negotiating processes through which organisational structures are reproduced are shaped by, and in turn shape, the prevailing pattern of power relations within an organisation. The latter generates a framework of unequally distributed capacities and opportunities among organisational personnel for reconstructing the structural forms through which they order their social relationships. In this way, the 'negotiated order'[20] model of organisation admits that all participants do not enter into negotiating processes from an equal position. Rather, they enjoy differentially distributed advantages in terms of their access to and control over scarce organisational resources – such as capital, manpower, technology, information and legitimating symbols – and the relative skill with which these are deployed to attain preferred decisional outcomes. However, it does maintain that the distribution of power, and the opportunity it affords to shape organisational design decisions, is far from being fixed and immutable. Indeed, the negotiated order model of organisation is based on the principle that power relations, and the opportunities which they provide to engage in the restructuring of organisational order, are essentially unstable and fluid structures that are always prone to degenerate as the balance of power between the plurality of interests which constitutes the organisation's political system fragments and changes. The hierarchical character of power relations within and between organisations is afforded some degree of recognition. Yet, its explanatory significance is downgraded in favour of a conception of power that concentrates on the negotiating processes through which organisational order is continually reworked and transformed.

Insofar as we can draw any direct and explicit policy recommendations from the characterisation and explanation of management structures and processes presented by the political perspective, these usually take the form of emphasising the potential improvement in the political skills and techniques of managers afforded by a deeper understanding of power conflicts and their implications for effective organisational designs.[21] Increased managerial awareness of, and sensitivity to, the subtle and pervasive political processes through which organisational change is negotiated is seen to facilitate the implementation of more effective forms of managerial control. This is so to the extent that they allow a more realistic appreciation of the obstacles that are likely to stand in the way of the achievement of preferred outcomes and a more grounded stock of recipes for removing them. The design, implementation and evaluation of alternative structural forms is likely to remain ineffective as long as it refuses to take sufficient cognisance of the political processes in which these activities are necessarily and unavoidably embedded.

Examples of sociological research on management from within the political perspective date back to the early 1950s – as found in Dalton's[22] pioneering study of the constantly shifting balance of power within and between managerial cliques and its impact on organisational innovation. The series of classic case studies on the dynamics of bureaucratic change, and the crucial role of internal power struggles between managers in shaping the change process, which were carried out between the mid-1950s and the mid-1960s, also stand testimony to the sociological value of the political perspective.[23] A later generation of researchers have further developed the analytical power and empirical utility of the political perspective by focusing upon the role of 'strategic choice' in shaping organisational structures; they have also emphasised the explanatory significance of the ideological commitments, material interests and political power of dominant coalitions in ensuring the implementation of preferred structural designs.[24] This later work has also highlighted the critical importance of analysing movements in the broader institutional context in which particular organisational units are located and their effect on internal political processes for developing a more sophisticated explanation of organisational change.

Yet, it is in relation to this area – that is, the interaction between institutional context and managerial power politics, and its implications for a more systematic understanding of the link between power relations and organisational change – that criticisms of the political perspectives have been most strongly voiced.[25] These criticisms relate both to the pluralistic conception of power relations that has informed the work of researchers working within the political perspective and to the relative neglect of the institutionalised structures of power and control contained within the encompassing political economy in which specific organisational units are deemed to operate. Thus, Willmott contends that:

> the pluralist perspective is still limited to the analysis of the mobilization of power resources by a variety of groups within organizations whose institutional formation is largely taken for granted. For although this highlights the significance of structural power differentials and conflicts of interests within organizations, the pluralist perspective offers little or no explanation of the distribution of power. Nor, relatedly, does it attend to the institutionalization of relations of power in the structures of work organization.[26]

It is this lack of attention to the institutional formation of intra-organisational power struggles, and its role in structuring the political processes through which resources are mobilised and structural designs transformed, which has provided the catalyst for formulating a critical perspective on management.

THE CRITICAL PERSPECTIVE

The critical perspective conceptualises management as a control mechanism that functions to fulfil the economic imperatives imposed by a capitalist mode of production and to disseminate the ideological frameworks through which these structural realities can be obscured. Managerial structures and strategies are treated as the instruments through which the economic and political interests of a ruling class within a specific mode of production are advanced and protected. The dominant economic imperative that management have to realise is the need to achieve a sufficient degree of control over the production process necessary to secure the efficient extraction of surplus value and corresponding levels of profitability that it guarantees. The overriding ideological demand they have to meet is the need to maintain the subordinate position of labour within the production process so that potential or actual resistance on the part of the former is minimised and contained within accepted institutional parameters.

This characterisation of management is logically tied to a Marxist approach to organisational analysis, which attempts to link the routine organisational work in which managers are engaged to the determining structure of production relations in which it takes place. This approach does not deny the practical relevance or explanatory significance of political conflicts within management (and between management and other groups) for an understanding or organisational outcomes and their impact on the everyday lives of participants. However, it does contend that these intra-organisational political processes are subordinate to – both in analytical and practical terms – the encompassing structure of capitalist production relations in which they are embedded and the functional imperatives that have to be met to ensure the latter survives as a viable socio-economic system.

In this way, both managerial personnel and the organisational designs they construct and maintain are treated as direct products of the socio-economic system under which they function as identifiable social groups and institutional units. The former are regarded as agents for, or bearers of, an economic logic that demands that labour is controlled and directed in the furtherance of sectional interests it would otherwise reject and overthrow. The latter provide the organisational means through which this task can be achieved in the form of material inducements, ideological appeals and administrative arrangements that prevent or contain workers' resistance and will incorporate them within a cultural and symbolic framework that literally 'mystifies' the structural realities to which they are subjected.

Such an interpretation recognises the existence of poorly integrated and inconsistent organisational designs that can be 'dysfunctional' from the viewpoint of achieving effective managerial control. Indeed, the major effort of researchers working within the critical tradition over the last few years or so has been directed towards the internal contradictions that are unavoidably contained within the strategies and structures of organisational control implemented by management.[27] In turn, these contradictory tendencies are seen to provide the source of successive waves of further managerial restructuring that attempt to eradicate the tensions which these conflicting objectives or principles cause, but merely succeed in exacerbating the original problems they were meant to solve.[28] The most important of these contradictions is seen to reside in the simultaneous desire for control over and co-operation from labour, and the parallel implementation of structural and ideological mechanisms (such as more coercive supervisory methods and co-operative ideological appeals) which ensure that these objectives are simultaneously negated.[29]

To the extent that any clear prescriptive managerial implications can be drawn from the critical perspective, these are expressed in terms of developing a deeper appreciation of management's role in regulating the institutionalised conflict of interest between capital and labour, as well as an increasing awareness of the contradictory strains and pressures this imposes on individual managers.[30] The latter are seen to be exposed to increasing pressure and tension due to the extraordinary strain the single-minded pursuit of the imperative of capital accumulation places on the successful performance of their conflict-regulating role. The requirement to maintain a delicate balance between the subordination of labour through structural control and the incorporation of labour through material and ideological inducement is threatened by those technological and organisational developments generated by the logic of capital accumulation.

These pressures are thought likely to make the position of management within the class structure of capitalist society even more difficult to sustain.[31] The logic of capital accumulation requires the limitation, if not dismantling, of any structural or ideological impediments that may result from a strategy of labour incorporation – life-time employment systems, high relative wage levels, good working conditions, consultative arrangements, paternalistic ideological appeals, etc. But it also threatens to reduce most managerial and supervisory personnel to exactly the same social and organisational status as that of subordinate labour.[32] As a result, managers become subjected to the same material deprivations and structural constraints – that is, deskilling processes – previously reserved for shop-floor workers, such as short-term employment contracts and rationalised systems of work control.[33] The impact of these developments on forms of class consciousness and action among middle managers and supervisors is a matter of some considerable debate within the critical tradition.[34] However, there seems to be general agreement that they will have a destablising effect on any ideological and political compromises that have been concocted to cope with the severe problems created by the contradictory class location of management in contemporary capitalist societies.[35] Thus, both in terms of its class location and organisational function within a capitalist mode of production, critical theorists present a view of management as an ideological mystification and institutional compromise that is unlikely to survive the technological, economic and social upheavals occasioned by the culmination of the workings of the 'inner logic' of capitalist development at the close of the twentieth century. The long-predicted end of management[36] is confirmed through a form of intellectual analysis that is itself underwritten by a watertight historical guarantee.

We find the clearest expression of the growing influence of a critical perspective within the sociology of management in that series of theoretical analyses and empirical studies of the labour process in capitalist societies set in motion by Braverman's[37] pioneering attempt to restate the superiority of a Marxist approach to the dynamics of work organisation and control. This work has been conducted over a wide range of issues,[38] but its main theoretical and substantive significance from the viewpoint of the sociology of management is the marked shift in emphasis away from a functionalist analysis towards a dialectical approach, and the considerable variation, not to say contradiction, in managerial control strategies and structures this has revealed.[39] This shift of emphasis has resulted in less attention being directed towards the formulation of an abstract and formalistic account of the structural imperatives that impose themselves on capitalist forms of work organisation and the functional role of management in fulfilling them. In its place, a view of management as a mechanism that mediates between external economic constraints and internal work designs has been developed. This mechanism, it is further maintained, consists of ideas, techniques, methods and practices related to the effective control of work performance that necessarily contain incomplete and contradictory recipes for action which produce unanticipated and unwelcome outcomes. At the same time, this model of management as a mediating mechanism which necessarily contains complex and contradictory recipes for action is further complicated by a clearer recognition of the multifarious forms of worker resistance that are mobilised in response to the implementation of innovative control systems. A growing realisation that 'the linkage between the logic of capital accumulation and transformations of the labour process is an indirect and varying one'[40] has provided the catalyst for a fundamental reworking of a model of management that is much more voluntaristic and pluralistic in its theoretical approach than that suggested by Braverman.

Nevertheless, an unresolved theoretical tension between a structuralist view of management – as a functional mechanism ensuring the maximisation of surplus value – and a dialectical interpretation highlighting the inevitable ruptures occurring between macro-level economic imperatives and micro-level control systems, remains at the conceptual core of the labour process approach.

The theoretical perspectives reviewed in this section signify the development of a sociology of management that is much more closely attuned to the inherent complexity and diversity of the social practices embedded within such a crucial social institution. However, an increasing awareness of, and receptiveness to, the dynamic quality of managerial practices has not resolved a number of crucial problems that confront any attempt to construct a coherent and integrated sociology of management. In certain respects, these problems have been exacerbated as sociologists have moved away from the overdeterministic predilections of structural analysis and

Table 1.1 Sociological perspectives on management

	Subject matter	Explanatory model	Policy strategy
1. Technical perspective	Rationally designed tool for the realisation of instrumental objectives	Systems theory	Enhanced effectiveness of structural design
2. Political perspective	Negotiated social process for the regulation of interest group conflict	Action theory	Improved negotiating skills for practitioners
3. Critical perspective	Control mechanism geared to the extraction of maximum surplus value	Marxist theory	Liberate practitioners from distorted view of social reality

welcomed the relief from abstract formalisation that a more historically oriented approach seemed to provide. These problems are discussed in the following section, while Table 1.1 provides a summary of the theoretical perspectives outlined in this section.

UNRESOLVED PROBLEMS

Four major unresolved problems arise out of the review conducted in the previous section. First, the failure to develop an integrated analytical framework linking together the study of managerial behaviour, organisational structure and institutional context within one perspective. Second, the tendency to fall back upon either structural determination or strategic choice in the face of seemingly overwhelming evidence as to the explanatory primacy of either. Third, the recourse to a functionalist explanatory logic that treats managers as the agents or bearers of social forces that contend in a wider institutional arena of which they have little or no theoretical knowledge, and treats managerial processes and systems as epiphenomena of 'deep structures' that develop according to their own logic within this arena. Fourth, and consequent upon the previous three points, the consistent failure to recognise the unavoidable dilemmas of managerial practice and their deep-seated implications for a form of sociological analysis which, whatever its particular theoretical bent, still remains wedded to a rational model of managerial action.

Sociological research on management has tended to proceed in an extremely *ad hoc* and fragmented manner with, until of late, little attempt to integrate the various levels of analysis at which it has been pursued. Thus, studies[41] of managerial work have progressed from a somewhat limited focus on task analysis and job characteristics to a 'political sociology'[42] approach that examines the key role played by certain managers in negotiating organisational order. However, studies such as these remain trapped within an organisational setting in which there is very little, if any, attempt to relate internal political processes to the broader institutional framework that shapes them. The technical analysis of organisational structure has made some belated attempt to link institutional change to redesign processes, but the relationship is theorised in terms of a set of restricted 'environmental contingencies' (such as market demand

and technical pressures) which impinge on managerial behaviour without any reference to the source of the latter in macro-level developments. In short, the sociological analysis of management is characterised by research effort conducted at a multiplicity of analytical levels, and shows little signs of achieving even a partial integration of the fragmented theoretical insights and empirical illustrations these studies reveal.

An understandable, if unfortunate, response in the face of this analytical fragmentation and empirical diversity is to fall back on a form of intellectual monotheism. This asserts the universal truth of one particular theoretical interpretation of the reality of managerial existence. It may express itself in various philosophical and conceptual guises, but it usually boils down to a Hobson's choice between seeing managers as bearers of structural forces over which they have little or no control or viewing them as free agents relatively unconstrained by prevailing socio-economic conditions. In either case, a recourse to a functionalist explanatory logic of some kind or another usually follows, even if this is modified in certain respects by reference to an extremely restricted area of choice or to the minimum constraint introduced by a consideration of environmental factors.

The recourse to functionalism seems to be irresistible once we move from a description of, to an explanation for, those characteristics that are seen to constitute the essence of managerial existence. From the point of view of the technical perspective, managers are treated as the agents for a formal or instrumental rationality focused on design faults that they may fail to appreciate and enact to its fullest extent in specific situations, but which will impose itself upon them eventually. Within the political perspective, a different kind of rationality prevails – one dominated by considerations of short-term political advantage and power within the employing organisation. But it tends to reduce managers to the status of ciphers for micro-level processes of which they possess little understanding and even less control. For those operating within the critical perspective, managers are best seen as merchants of morality. They act as the conduits for an economic logic that has to be obscured, hidden and distorted in some way or another through the promulgation of various ideological mystifications.

In each case managers simply become the agents for functional imperatives that originate outside the social practice in which they are routinely engaged. As the carriers of an instrumental rationality or the public front-men for private organisational politicking or the playthings of inexorable social forces, they lose any viable claim to self-interpretation and sustainable cultural identity. This results in a denial of the unavoidable ethical and political dilemmas that managers confront in the performance of a social practice that is necessarily characterised by a considerable degree of empirical diversity, political uncertainty and moral ambiguity. An over-socialised model of management leads to a form of sociological analysis in which the often fragmented, constrained and conservative quality of managerial conduct becomes overlaid by a theoretical gloss. This reflects these characteristics in the form of an idealised image that seems to bear little relationship to the reality it purports to represent.

Consequently, taken in isolation, none of the three analytical perspectives we have discussed exhibits a sufficient degree of theoretical and methodological sensitivity to the ambiguities of managerial practice.

The technical perspective assumes that, in the long run, managerial behaviour will be dominated by a neutral means-oriented rationality, even if temporary deviations from this universal norm will sometimes be encountered in specific situations. Indeed, its focus on the key relationship between managerial task activity and formal structure[43] is motivated by a concern to reassert the determining force of a functionalist imperative that imposes itself on management action, but may need to be given a helping hand in cases of transient organisational pathology. The pro-active role of managers in generating and sustaining the organisational ambiguities and uncertainties they face is minimising to the point of virtual analytical extinction. It is recognised only as an obstacle that occasionally gets in the way of a more logical relationship between organisational design and environmental demands. The contribution of conflicting interests and values institutionalised within the wider society to the development of intra-organisational strains and tensions is reduced to a cluster of environmental pressures that are presumed to structure managerial decisions over organisational design. In turn, these decisions are regarded as outcomes of a procedure in which the relationship between organisational means and ends is treated as a particular example of a more general process that brings resources and objectives into rational alignment.

The inadequacies of a rational model of managerial decision-making provide the critical point of entry for those advocating a political perspective on managerial behaviour and organisation. However, the conception of politics which informs this approach is restricted to a concern with the way in which resource allocation processes are manipulated by non-rational considerations related to sectional interests and values – particularly those held by the dominant coalition within the organisation's managerial élite.[44] Politics is deemed to be synonymous with politicking. Any broader theoretical or practical concern with the general moral dilemmas and principles that may direct managerial behaviour, especially in conflict situations, is missing. As a result, the force of Anthony's argument that 'because they (managers) are concerned with social and political relationships in organisations, they have a real concern with moral relationships'[45] is completely lost within a debunking methodology that seeks to expose the sectional interests lying behind professed commitments to normative principles of justice, fairness and equality. Once more, the initial recognition of complexity and subtlety is overpowered by the search for *the* determining force necessary to explain managerial behaviour and organisation.

The reductionist tendency evident within the political perspective neatly dovetails with the inclination of critical theorists to assume that managerial conduct is driven by an inexorable economic logic that can be resisted only at the cost of organisational destruction. The intra-organisational focus of the technical and political perspectives is superseded by a political economy of managerial behaviour which contemptuously sweeps aside any remaining concern with the explanatory role of moral values and commitments. In its place we find a model of the managerial organisation as a hierarchical control system in which multiple levels of managerial activity are closely conditioned by a centrally determined and co-ordinated strategy of capital accumulation. Within this model, individual managers are treated as the principal 'bearers' of the inner economic logic at work within capitalism:

> when examined from this perspective, the question of whether individual managers act with the intention of securing or advancing the interest of capital, or accept this account of their work, is irrelevant . . . managerial work is seen to be primarily governed by the structure of relations of production that it

'bears'. . . . As agents of capital, managers are seen to develop and/or implement strategies and structures that ensure the productive subordination of labour to the demands of capital. Fundamentally, managerial work is thus understood to involve creating and maintaining a structure of relationships in which those who are 'in control' act in the interests of capital.[46]

Yet, this model of managerial organisation as a tightly sprung control system that programmes the thinking and conduct of individual managers at all levels receives little support from the actual empirical research carried out on the relationship – or lack of it – between corporate strategy and labour management strategy.[47] This literature will be discussed in greater detail in the next chapter. What it does reveal, however, is that the underlying commitment to a highly deterministic and rationalistic account of managerial strategy contained within the critical perspective severely limits its capacity to cope with the reality of a process shot through with inconsistency and incrementalism. Critical theorists[48] recognise the reality of inevitable contradictions and breaks within and between different forms and levels of control. Nevertheless, the theoretical framework they rely upon is based on a logic of explanation that marginalises the significance of these complexities and their implications for the kind of conceptual equipment we need for constructing more sensitive accounts of managers' efforts to organise and control productive activity.

The three perspectives discussed so far each reveal a crucial aspect of management practice. The technical perspective focuses on the formal administrative structures through which managers attempt to co-ordinate organisational behaviour. The political perspective highlights the social processes through which these structures are enacted; and the critical perspective emphasises the wider material interests to which the latter are subordinated. However, we lack a general conceptual framework in which these important, but partial, insights can be integrated in a systematic and coherent fashion. An attempt will be made to provide such a framework in the next section.

THE PRACTICE PERSPECTIVE

The preceding assessment of the three sociological perspectives that have informed our thinking about managerial behaviour and organisation suggests the need for a substantial reconsideration. We must look more carefully at the conceptual equipment through which we approach the theoretical, methodological and ideological issues that crystallise in the general theme of management. What we require is an approach that is sensitive to the empirical diversity and social ambiguity of those managerial practices through which collective social action becomes sufficiently structured to take on a coherent and reasonably stable institutional shape in the form of work organisations. This approach must also be able to link together the behavioural, organisational and institutional levels of analysis that are evident in the sociology of management. In this way, the interrelationships between managerial work, control strategies and macro-structural constraints can become more systematically theorised.

In recent years there has begun to emerge an approach that seems to provide a more promising response to these problems. This does not require an unquestioned theoretical commitment to a conception of management as an administrative structure *or* a sociopolitical process *or* a control mechanism. Instead, it attempts to integrate each of these analytical components within a view of management as a social practice. Over the last ten years or so this perspective on management as a social practice has emerged in the work of researchers such as Burns,[49] Tomlinson,[50] Batstone[51] and Anthony.[52] Their work has highlighted the ethical and political dilemmas that managers necessarily face in their struggle to cope with the inherent complexity and contradictions of work organisations. It has also served to emphasise the importance of understanding the social processes whereby these dilemmas are reflected in the makeshift, and often internally contradictory, assemblies of practices that constitute contemporary work organisations as *bricolages* of partially articulated and half-digested sets of principles or rationalities.[53]

Recently, Tomlinson has provided a theoretical characterisation of management as consisting of:

the containment of separate and other contradictory practices – a matter of keeping the show on the road. Management is then seen as facing such problems as 'How can the practices of sub-agency A be made compatible with those of B?' and 'How can the decisions of C be summarised in their negative impact on D?' rather than how the practices of A, B, C, and D can be subordinated to the goals of the enterprise.[54]

In this way, management is treated as a process or activity aimed at the continual recoupling or smoothing over of diverse and complex practices always prone to disengagement and fragmentation. It is based on the, usually contested, capacity to control the institutional mechanisms through which some degree of overall co-ordination and integration of social interaction can be secured. This implies a rather different view of work organisations to that conveyed in the more orthodox approaches we reviewed earlier in this chapter. Within the practice perspective, work organisations are seen as points of intersection for a wide range of social practices that are subjected to various strategies of institutional combination and recombination. This offers a more realistic and flexible conception than that which treats organisations as rigidly structured social units subordinated to the performance of an essential function within the economic, technical, administrative or political imperatives imposed by a particular socio-economic sector or system. It also indicates that work organisations are based on operating principles and rationales that generate both structural and processual contradictions that will be reflected within management practice. Not only will managers be called upon to secure organisational discipline and membership consent simultaneously, but they will also be internally divided, both between and within different specialisms, over how these mutually incompatible objectives are to be achieved.[55]

It may be appropriate at this point to offer a rather more formalised specification of the practice perspective which builds on recent development of the concept of social practice within social and political analysis, before moving on to its broader implications for the sociology of management. This can be achieved in three stages: first, by providing a general theoretical characterisation of the concept of social practice; second, by elaborating upon this basic conception in the form of a crucial distinction between primary and secondary social practices; and third, by developing this distinction in regard of management as a particular type of secondary social practice.

The concept of social practice has figured prominently in the recent contributions of a number of writers and researchers in the fields of philosophy, anthropology, sociology, organisational studies and economics.[56] Harris provides a useful definition of the concept, which can form the starting point for further elaboration. To engage in a social practice involves:

> engaging in a class of actions which are intelligible in and through the concepts which inform them, which have to be understood as directed towards ends which all members of the community of practitioners share, and is defined through the means adopted to the achievement of those ends which are to be understood as determined by the conditions under which the practice is undertaken.[57]

From this basic definition, it is possible to identify five interrelated conceptual components that together form the analytical framework for organising our thinking about management that is on offer within this chapter. Conceptualising management as an identifiable social practice requires that five distinct, but interrelated, factors are specified:

1. The class of actions in which practitioners are engaged as members of that community or practice.
2. The concepts through which certain shared aims or problems are identified in a meaningful way by practitioners as a basis for engaging in reciprocal interaction.
3. The shared aims or problems to which the practice is directed as communicated in the practitioners' conceptual vocabulary.
4. The means or resources (both material and symbolic) through which achievement of these meaningful projects is pursued.
5. The situational conditions or constraints under which these reciprocated activities, the resources they require, and the relationships they engender between practitioners, are shaped and directed.

All social situations are constituted through communities of practitioners related to each other by virtue of the concepts internal to the practices in which they are engaged and by the shared resources and conditions under which they are undertaken. However, practices have to be assembled in various ways by other practices to form distinctive and viable institutions. The distinction between primary and secondary social practices provides further insight into the process whereby this assembly and regulation is managed. Primary social practices are aimed at transforming the environmental circumstances in which human life is carried on through the production of goods, services and the ideas that inform our conceptions of them.[58]

Secondary social practices are directed at achieving overall integration and co-ordination of primary social practices through the design, implementation and monitoring of various judicial, political and administrative mechanisms. The latter serve to assemble the diverse and complex array of primary practices in which human populations are necessarily involved into institutional structures that exhibit a minimum degree of normative coherence, social cohesion and temporal continuity.

Considered in these terms, management can be broadly defined as that secondary social practice through which administrative regulation and control is established and maintained over those activities and relationships in which non-managerial practitioners are engaged by virtue of their membership of communities of primary productive practice. It is directed at assembling diverse and complex productive practices into institutional structures that exhibit an acceptable degree of conceptual and material coherence. This is achieved through the application of a range of physical and symbolic resources, and the implementation of various co-ordinating mechanisms through which incipient fragmentation and decay can be temporarily resisted. Consequently, management constitutes both a mechanism through which conflict over the possession and control of resources necessary for primary productive activity can be, at least temporarily, regulated and a process which provides a medium for struggle over the institutional arrangements through which this regulation is achieved.

This approach offers three main theoretical advantages over those discussed earlier in this chapter. First, it provides a conceptual synthesis of three key aspects of management that have previously been isolated from each other – that is, technique, process and mechanism. It realises this synthesis by conceptually reworking and recombining these elements within a model of management as a social unit of reciprocal interaction geared to the task of assembling productive practices through the process of organisational structuring. Within the latter, a framework of rules, resources and supporting rationales will be constructed to provide the mechanisms by which managers strive to exert a satisfactory degree of control over and commitment from primary producers.

Second, it rejects the more orthodox treatment of management as a unitary control device that ensures the single-minded pursuit of an unambiguous technical, political or ideological imperative to which all aspects of social action, including managerial action, must be rigidly subordinated. In its place, the practice framework suggests that the task of management is to ensure a viable degree of overall co-ordination and control of diverse primary productive practices that contain very powerful centrifugal forces pushing in the direction of even greater complexity and fragmentation. It also indicates that, in pursuing this institutional containment and regulation, managerial practitioners will have to rely on a wide range of specialised mechanisms and supporting rationales to achieve their aims which may come into conflict with one another.

The interests of those who own and/or control the strategic material resources and instruments necessary for primary productive activity in any society are likely to be the most influential consideration informing management's design and implementation of the various integrative mechanisms through which overall assembly and regulation may be attempted. However, managers will also be exposed to alternative sources of pressure and demands that will shape the particular mechanisms and rationales they follow in attempting to recouple diverse primary productive practices that have become, or are in danger of becoming, disengaged. As such, they will be required to develop an acceptable, and necessarily shifting, *modus vivendi* between competing rationales, each with their own internal logics and supporting justifications.[59]

Third, the approach outlined in this section provides an integrated conceptual framework that can interrelate behavioural, organisational and institutional levels of analysis without falling prey to the deterministic functionalist analysis that alternative perspectives retreat into when faced with the complexity of managerial existence. This is achieved by focusing upon the range of regulative and co-ordinating strategies managers must rely upon to organise productive practices and the problems their usage presents to the continued integrity and viability of the institutional structures in which they are loosely grounded. In this way, managerial behaviour inevitably reflects the tension that necessarily arises between maintaining the long-term integrity and viability of the institutionalised control systems on which managers rely to achieve overall integration and the operational requirement for the application of specific devices and understandings that undermine the coherence and stability of the former. The contradiction between a bureaucratic logic that demands strict adherence to the rules of imperative co-ordination and an operational practice that requires the utilisation of devices, techniques and agreements which have no place within the former, provides the focal point for the conceptual framework we have developed in this section.[60] This contradiction also permits a clearer identification of the crucial role managers play in mediating between the internal pressures exerted by organisational stakeholders and the external demands issuing from coalitions located in the interorganisational network of which their organisation is a part.

CONCLUSION

The three views of management embodied in the analytical perspectives discussed in the earlier sections of this chapter – as a formal structure, a negotiated social order and a control function – can be brought together in a conception of management practice as a loosely connected set of mechanisms, processes and strategies directed at the assembly of other practices concerned with the production of goods, services and ideas that transform the environment we inhabit. The connections between these three aspects of management practice, such as they are, are most clearly revealed when transformations in the situational conditions under which productive practices are assembled and regulated erode the traditional organisational arrangements on which managers have relied. Consequently, changes to the conceptual and material circumstances under which specific types of organisational design and control are implemented by managers – such as new management philosophies, innovative production technologies and the discovery of alternative markets – are likely to provide the catalyst for reconsidering and reworking accepted arrangements.

Thus, the periods during which substantial organisational re-structuring has to be initiated by managers against a backdrop of situational change are likely to prove most revealing in terms of the underlying tensions that are released between the logic of bureau-cratic control and the operational demand for coping devices that radically undermine the former. It is also at this juncture that the need for managers to maintain a proper balance between their concern for the long-term integrity and viability of organisational machinery and the immediacy of short-term pressures for workable solutions to everyday crises becomes most pressing. In this context, the difficulties that many managers often face in reconciling the conflict between an instrumental rationality, which demands strict adherance to the protection of organisational means deemed neces-sary for survival, and a substantive rationality, which calls for an authentic concern with the moral ends to which managerial action ought to be directed, can become acute. This also provides further illustration of the intellectual poverty and practical impotency of a conception of management that treats its practitioners as clinical technicians or as mini-Machiavellis or as prisoners of a structural logic that they cannot recognise, much less understand. In its place, it suggests that management practice consists of a complex web of interrelationships between the technical, political and moral dimen-sions of managerial conduct oriented to the assembly of those recalcitrant resources that enter into productive activity. Within this general perspective, we can develop a view of individual managers as practitioners of an art that requires the possession and application of skills enabling them to cope with the contradictory demands and pressures of resources that stubbornly resist efforts to contain them within prescribed limits.

The analysis that follows in the rest of this book is intended to improve our understanding of the unavoidable dilemmas and problems encountered in the attempt to assemble and maintain workable institutional structures that reflect the uncertainties and ambiguities of the practices through which they are constructed. Managers cannot avoid these uncertainties and ambiguities; in-deed, the very nature of what they do expresses the contingent and paradoxical quality of human action, which simultaneously denies and attempts to cope with the seemingly intractable problems that prevent them creating and sustaining order in the face of chaos. The public rhetoric of technocratic ideology conveys a Platonic image of the manager as a rational planner and controller of an organisational machine that is infinitely adaptable to rapidly changing conditions. The private language suggests a very different picture – somebody struggling to come to terms with a reality that stubbornly refuses to conform to this organisational blueprint or to fit the universal categories and laws it specifies. It is time that the credibility gap between public image and private reality was bridged by a theoretical perspective focused on the unavoidable dilemmas managers have to contend with in their struggle to construct a workable compromise between structural constraints and human recalcitrance.

This exploration of the contribution management has made to the process of structuring is pursued in relation to a number of crucial themes that recur in the sociology of management. First, we need to achieve a better understanding of the historical development of the various forms of organisational control managers have tried to implement in different institutional settings as a means of securing effective structuring of work performance. Second, we must examine the impact of these forms of control on the nature and quality of managerial work in order to realise a more rounded and sensitive appreciation of its inherent dilemmas and the manner in which they are contained. Third, we shall review the response this organisational work has elicited from those subjected to the mechanisms of control, and do this with particular reference to the generation and regulation of industrial conflict within the employment relationship. Fourth, we shall discuss the implications of the previous analysis for the location and role of managerial groups within the class structure of advanced societies. Finally, the insights derived from the exploration of managerial structuring conducted above will provide the basis for a more general assessment of the alternative futures managers face in a world that is unlikely to become completely àmenable to their efforts to eradicate its inherent uncertainties and perversities.

The next chapter reviews and evaluates those sociological studies that have focused on the various attempts made by succeeding generations of managers, under a variety of situational conditions, to assemble and control productive labour in the light of the theoretical perspective on management we have looked at in this chapter.

REFERENCES

1. Giddens uses this term to refer to any social order which has moved beyond 'simple market society' and as a way of avoiding many of the difficulties associated with the concept of 'industrial society'. On this point see Giddens, A., *The Class Structure of the Advanced Societies* (Hutchinson, London, 1973) pp. 141–3.

2. This point is most forcefully argued in Carter, R., *Capitalism, Class Conflict and the New Middle Class* (Routledge and Kegan Paul, London, 1985).

3. For a brief illustration of this problem see Lowe, E.A., 'Introduction' to 'Critical Perspectives on Management Studies and Management Science', *Journal of Management Studies* Special Issue, vol. 21, No. 3, (1984).

4. The arguments developed in this chapter are an extension of some of those outlined in Reed, M., *Redirections in Organizational Analysis* (Tavistock, London, 1985).

5. On this point, see Donaldson's recent attempt to reconstruct a functionalist organisation theory based on a more subtle and sophisticated classification of functional imperatives in Donaldson, R., *In Defence of Organisation Theory: A Reply to the Critics* (Cambridge University Press, Cambridge, 1985).

6. For an excellent review of this approach see Massie, J., 'Management Theory', in March, J. (ed.), *The Handbook of Organizations* (Rand McNally, New York, 1965).

7. The positivistic assumptions underlying the classical approach and their ideological correlates are highlighted in Waldo, D., *The Administrative State* (Knopf, New York, 1948); Wolin, S., *Politics and Vision* (Allen & Unwin, London, 1961); Mouzelis, N., *Organisation and Bureaucracy* (Routledge and Kegan Paul, London, 1967).

8. For an elaboration of this point and its operational significance see Lupton, T., *Management and the Social Services* (Penguin, London, 2nd edition, 1983).

9. For specific examples of this critique see Etzioni, A., *Modern Organisations* (Prentice-Hall, Englewood Cliffs, New Jersey, 1964); Woodward, J., *Industrial Organisation: Theory and Practice* (Oxford University Press, London, 1965); Thompson, J.D., *Organizations in Action* (McGraw-Hill, New York, 1967).

10. On this point see Mintzberg, H., *The Nature of Managerial Work* (Harper and Row, New York, 1973).

11. Etzioni, A., *A Comparative Analysis of Complex Organizations* (Free Press, New York, 2nd edition, 1975).

12. Thompson, J.D., op. cit., (1967).

13. Lawrence, P.R. and Lorsch, J.W., *Organization and Environment* (Harvard University Press, Cambridge, Mass., 1967).

14. Pugh, D.S. and Hickson, D.J., *Organisation Structure in its Context:*

The Aston Programme I, (Saxon House, Farnborough, 1976).

15. Donaldson attempts to resolve this inconsistency, but his analysis is forced back on to the deterministic explanatory logic that informs systems theory. On this point see Donaldson, R., op. cit.

16. This term was originally used by Child to efer to that group within the internal management structure who retain the capacity to make key decisions over investment, allocation, reorganisation, etc. On this point see Child, J., 'Organisational structure, environment and performance', *Sociology*, vol. 6, No. 1, (1972), pp. 2–22. Further elaborations and usages of the concept will be discussed in Chapter five.

17. The phrase is taken from Burns, T., 'A comparative study of administrative structure and organisational processes in selected areas of the national health service', *Social Science Research Council Report*, Report Number HRP 6725, (1982).

18. For a general outline of this approach see Silverman, D., *The Theory of Organisations* (Heinemann, London, 1970).

19. Elger, A., 'Industrial organizations: a processual perspective', in McKinley, J.B. (ed.), *Processing People: Cases in Organizational Behaviour* (Holt, Rinehart and Winston, New York, 1975), p. 97.

20. For a further elaboration of this model see Strauss, A., *et al.*, 'The hospital and its negotiated order', in Friedson, E. (ed.), *The Hospital in Modern Society* (Macmillan, New York, 1963).

21. For a recent example of attempts to develop this aspect of the political model see Lee, R. and Lawrence, P., *Organisational Behaviour: Politics at Work* (Hutchinson, London, 1985).

22. Dalton, M., *Men Who Manage* (John Wiley and Son, New York, 1959).

23. Selznick, P., *TVA and the Grass Roots* (University of California Press, Berkeley, 1949); Gouldner, A., *Patterns of Industrial Bureaucracy* (Collier-Macmillan, New York, 1954); and *Wildcat Strike* (Antioch Press, New York, 1954); Blau, P., *The Dynamics of Bureaucracy* (University of Chicago Press, Chicago, 1955); Burns, T. and Stalker, G.M., *The Management of Innovation* (Tavistock, London, 1961); Crozier, M., *The Bureaucratic Phenomenon* (University of Chicago Press, Chicago, 1964).

24. Child, J., 'Organisation: a choice for man', in Child, J. (ed.), *Man and Organisation* (Allen and Unwin, London, 1973); Pettigrew, A., *The Politics of Organisational Decision-Making* (Tavistock, London, 1973), and *The Awakening Giant* (Basil Blackwell, London, 1985); Pfeffer, J., *Power in Organisations* (Pitman, Massachusetts, 1981); Kotter, J.P., *Power in Management* (Amacon, New York, 1979) and *The General Managers* (Free Press, New York, 1982).

25. Day, R.A. and Day, J.V., 'A review of the current state of negotiated order theory: an appreciation and critique', *Sociological Quarterly*, vol. 18, No. 4, (1977), pp. 126–42; Whitley, R., 'Organisational control and the problem of order', *Social Science Information*, vol. 16, No. 2, (1977), pp. 169–89; Salaman, G., *Work Organisations: Resistance and Control* (Longman, London, 1979); Burrell, G. and Morgan, G.,

Sociological Paradigms and Organisational Analysis (Heinemann, London, 1979); Willmott, H.C., 'Images and ideals of managerial work: a critical examination of conceptual and empirical accounts', *Journal of Management Studies*, vol. 21, No. 3, (1984), pp. 349–68.
26. Willmott, H.C., op. cit., p. 361.
27. Benson, J.K., 'Organisations: a dialectical view', *Administrative Science Quarterly*, vol. 22, No. 1, (1977), pp. 1–21; Salaman, G., 'Towards a sociology of organisational structure', *Sociological Review*, vol. 26, No. 3, (1978), pp. 519–54; Littler, C.R., *The Development of the Labour Process in Capitalist Societies* (Heinemann, London, 1982).
28. For a number of specific illustrations of this general theme see Storey, J., *Managerial Prerogative and the Question of Control* (Routledge and Kegan Paul, London, 1983). This theme is further discussed in Chapter two.
29. This issue is dealt with at some length in Littler, C.R. and Salaman, G., *Class at Work: The Design, Allocation and Control of Jobs* (Batsford, London, 1984).
30. On this point see Fox, A., *Man Mismanagement* (Hutchinson, London, 2nd edition, 1985).
31. This issue will be dealt with at greater length in Chapter five.
32. This highly controversial thesis concerning the 'proletarianisation' of middle and lower level management has been most fully developed in Crompton, R. and Jones, G., *White Collar Proletariat: Deskilling and Gender in Clerical Work* (Macmillan, London, 1984).
33. A more subtle appreciation of 'managerial deskilling and reskilling' is to be found in Ray, C.A., 'Images of skill reconsidered: the conceptual deskilling of line managers', unpublished paper, Merrill College, University of California.
34. The new middle class or new working class interpretations of these developments are discussed in Chapter five.
35. On this point see Salaman, G., 'Managing the frontier of control', in Giddens, A. and Mackenzie, G. (eds.), *Social Class and the Division of Labour* (Cambridge University Press, Cambridge, 1982).
36. The phrase is taken from Fletcher, C., 'The end of management', in Child, J., op. cit., (1973).
37. Braverman, H., *Labour and Monopoly Capital: The Degradation of Work in the Twentieth Century* (Monthly Review Press, New York, 1974).
38. These are discussed in Thompson, P., *The Nature of Work* (Macmillan, London, 1983).
39. Recent studies that illustrate this point include Zimblast, A. (ed.), *Case Studies on the Labour Process* (Monthly Review Press, New York, 1979); Wood, S. (ed.), *The Degradation of Work* (Hutchinson, London, 1982); Knights, D. and Willmott, H.C. (eds.), *Managing the Labour Process* (Gower, London, 1986).
40. Littler, C.R., op. cit., (1982), p. 34.
41. These will be reviewed in Chapter three.
42. For two recent examples of this see Stewart, R., 'The nature of

management? A problem for management education', *Journal of Management Studies*, vol. 21, No. 3, (1984), pp. 321–30; and Mintzberg, H., 'The organisation of political arena', *Journal of Management Studies*, vol. 22, (1985), pp. 133–54.
43. On this point see Donaldson, L., op. cit., (1985).
44. Pettigrew's recent book on ICI is an excellent example of this approach. See Pettigrew, A., op. cit., (1985).
45. Anthony, P.D., *The Foundations of Management* (Tavistock, London, 1986), p. 186.
46. Willmott, H.C., op. cit., (1984), p. 362.
47. As discovered in Winkler, J.T., 'The ghost at the bargaining table: directors and industrial relations', *British Journal of Industrial Relations*, vol. 12, No. 2, (1974), pp. 191–212; Purcell, J. and Sissons, K., 'Strategies and practice in the management of industrial relations' in Bain, G. (ed.), *Industrial Relations in Britain* (Basil Blackwell, London, 1983); Gospel, H., 'The development of management organisation in industrial relations: a historical perspective', in Thurley, K. and Woods, S. (eds.), *Industrial Relations and Management Strategy* (Cambridge University Press, Cambridge, 1983); and 'Managerial structures and strategies: an introduction', in Gospel, H. and Littler, C.R. (eds.), *Managerial Strategies and Industrial Relations* (Heinemann, London, 1983); Rose, M. and Jones, B., 'Managerial strategy and trade union response in work re-organisation schemes at establishment level', in Knights, D., Willmott, H.C. and Collinson, D., *Job Redesign: Critical Perspectives on the Labour Process* (Gower, London, 1985).
48. This point is given particular emphasis in Storey, J., 'The means of management control', *Sociology*, vol. 19, No. 2, pp. 193–212.
49. Burns, T., *The BBC* (Macmillan, London, 1977).
50. Tomlinson, J., *Unequal Struggle: British Socialism and the Capitalist Enterprise* (Methuen, London, 1982).
51. Batstone, E., 'Management and industrial democracy' in *Industrial Democracy: International Views* (Social Science Research Council, London, 1978).
52. Anthony, P.D., op. cit., (1986).
53. The idea of the work organisation as constituting a *bricolage* of practices assembled on the basis of ambiguous and contradictory principles is developed in Burns, T., op. cit., (1982).
54. Tomlinson, J., op. cit., (1982), p. 128.
55. For a recent development of this point see Armstrong, P., 'Competition between the organisational professions and the evolution of management control strategies', in Thompson, K. (ed.), *Work, Employment and Unemployment: Perspectives on Work and Society* (Open University Press, Milton Keynes, 1984).
56. Bordieu, R., *Outline of a Theory of Practice* (Cambridge University Press, Cambridge, 1977); Giddens, A., *Central Problems in Social Theory* (Macmillan, London, 1979); Donzelot, J., *The Policing of Families* (Hutchinson, London, 1980); Parkin, F., *Marxism and Class Theory: A Bourgeois Critique* (Tavistock, London, 1979); MacIntyre,

A., *After Virtue: A Study in Moral Theory* (Duckworth, London, 1981); Runciman, W.G., 'On the tendency of human societies to form varieties', *London Review of Books*, 5 June 1986, pp. 16–18; Johnston, L., *Marxism, Class Analysis and Socialist Pluralism* (Allen and Unwin, London, 1986).
57. Harris, C.C., *Fundamental Concepts and the Sociological Enterprise* (Croom Helm, London, 1980), p. 29.
58. Ibid., pp. 64–5.
59. Empirical illustrations of this point are detailed in subsequent chapters.
60. Some managers, particularly those who have direct operational responsibility for productive activity, may find the tensions more pressing than others. It is assumed here that, to varying degrees, all managers experience them.

2

MANAGERIAL CONTROL

INTRODUCTION

Each of the theoretical perspectives discussed in the previous chapter regards control as *the* central process relevant to the sociological analysis of management. However, each perspective develops a characteristic approach to the analysis of managerial control, both in respect of the nature of the problem to which it is directed and the manner in which the latter is resolved.

This chapter will examine management control as a social process directed to the organisation of work relations in social situations characterised by conflict over both the ends of productive activity and the means through which they are secured. It will focus on the changing control strategies and structures through which management have attempted to organise productive activity undertaken by social groups that bring conflicting priorities and interests to the work situation. A more detailed consideration of the source of the latter within higher levels of socio-economic organisation above that of the work organisation and business enterprise will be postponed until Chapter five.

Before proceeding to a more systematic analysis of managerial control strategies and structures, we need to relate the problem of control to the previous discussion of theoretical perspectives on management. This will provide a background against which we can examine different forms of managerial control.

THE PROBLEM OF CONTROL

Each of the theoretical perspectives we have reviewed in the previous chapter shares a common assessment of the paramount theoretical and practical significance of managerial control. But the way in which they interpret the latter concept is subject to considerable variation, not to say dispute.

The technical perspective views the problem of control as ensuring appropriate organisational adaptation to environmentally induced disequilibrium in a situation where various non-rational considerations (such as the conflicting demands of different departments) must be overcome. Thus, the process of control is broken down into an interrelated set of mechanisms or procedures through which management can restructure the organisation to meet more effectively the demands and threats posed by its environment.[1]

The political perspective identifies the control problem as the need to regulate interest group conflict with sufficient skill and flexibility so as to permit the negotiation and re-negotiation of organisational order. This is deemed necessary because all organisational arrangements tend to fragment and dissolve in the face of complex developmental processes that undermine the integrity, viability and stability of formal control devices. Managers find it difficult to display sufficient skill in accommodating the competing claims and priorities which impinge on the development of work organisation in such a way that their operational viability and institutional identity can be preserved and defended.[2]

The critical perspective treats the problem of control as one of simultaneously securing and mystifying the exploitative relationship between a dominant and subordinate class whose interests are placed in a position of structured antagonism because of the conflicting priorities embedded in such a relationship.[3] It argues that those who gain most from the set-up that secures and maintains surplus value must be protected by a framework designed and implemented by specialists. In this way, subordinate groups, who might challenge their orders, can be made harmless.

The practice perspective attempts to rework and reintegrate each of these interpretations within a conception of managerial control as a loosely coupled network of co-ordinating practices geared to the assembly of productive activity. The latter is assumed to be based on the exclusive possession of productive resources and the struggle to realise conflicting interests which this generates.[4] These control practices are deemed necessary as a result of the diversity and complexity essential to large-scale productive activity dependent on advanced technology. They are also a consequence of the conflicts arising out of the exclusive possession and ownership of productive resources.

Within this general conception of managerial control, the practice framework also indicates that particular instances of work organisation will exhibit a range of co-ordinating practices that will contain internal contradictions. It also implies that the process of managerial control is a loose set of co-ordinating practices emerging out of the interaction between a wide range of factors within and without the work organisation as a social unit. Individuals and groups within management will be selectively subjected to the constraints imposed by the control practices they have helped to design and implement.

FORMS OF CONTROL

Most of the discussion about management control strategies and structures has focused on the changing forms of control that managers attempt to implement in a dynamic configuration of socio-economic conditions.[5] This has produced a range of typologies relating to different kinds of control systems and the contingent circumstances in which they are most likely to be effective from the viewpoint of the technical, political and economic constraints impinging on work organisations. These typologies have also figured very prominently in the efforts that have been made to explain the exact relationship between different forms of managerial control and the specific situational conditions in which they are most likely to be practised.

Analysts working within the technical perspective have attempted to develop control typologies linked to a range of environmental contingencies located at the level of an organisation's operational domain[6] or at the level of the wider social system as a whole. Woodward's[7] work is indicative of the former approach to the extent that it relates variations in the structure of the management control system to aspects of production technology and formal organisation. Etzioni's[8] threefold typology of organisational control systems – linking forms of managerial power to forms of lower participant involvement – is predicated on the assumption of organisational units performing specialised functional tasks for the inclusive social system in which they are located.

Thompson[9] provides a more integrated analytical framework in that he conceptually reworks many of the most significant technical studies on managerial control within a model of the work organisation as displaying three distinct levels of control – technical, managerial and institutional.[10] Technical control relates to problems of effective performance of basic operational tasks (e.g., materials processing). Managerial control refers to those processes that mediate between the technical core and those who use its products, while at the same time procuring resources necessary for operational activity. Institutional control highlights those activities concerned with securing ideological support from within the political domain in which the organisation is situated and justifying the claims it makes on scarce resources.

Within this three-level model of organisational control, Thompson argues that the managerial level plays an absolutely crucial role in mediating between the closed-system aspects of the technical core and the open-system logic of the institutional domain. The managerial control system mediates between the two extremes of a technical core, which demands minimum uncertainty by reducing the number of variables acting on it, and an institutional domain in which the intrusion of external variables and the intensified uncertainty this generates is indispensable for continued support. Management control systems, in this sense, balance the demands for operational stability and the pressures for environmental instability by 'ironing out some irregularities stemming from external sources, but also pressing the technical core for modifications as conditions alter'.[11]

This basic approach to the technical aspects of managerial control systems is developed further in the contributions to Lowe and Machin's[12] anthology. The latter reviews the transition in the management science literature on control from highly formalistic and rationalistic accounts of control structures to processual models relating patterns of environmental contingencies and organisational arrangements to managerial power struggles. This has produced a much more analytically sophisticated and sensitive analysis of the ideological assumptions that underpin control systems design and their grounding in power relations both within and without management.[13] As a consequence of this intellectual development, a shared interest in managerial control strategies as decision-making processes loosely coupling environmental contingencies, managerial politics and structural design has emerged in the technical and political perspectives.

Researchers working within the latter perspective have always been more acutely aware of the intimate relationship between forms of managerial control systems and the processes of managerial power politics in which they are embedded. Dalton's[14] insight into the subordination of formalised control structures to the disruptive impact of sectorial conflict within management pioneered a tradition of sociological research that revealed the hidden agendas that dramatically shape the process of organisational change. This tradition is clearly expressed by Burns,[15] who uncovered the complex processes whereby rational control systems are distorted by the long-term impact of substantive conflicts within management over access to resources that will critically affect the future direction of organisational development. Pettigrew's[16] focus on the degree of political skill exhibited by different individuals and groups within management in turning resource access to good political effect also reflects this tradition.

Increasingly, researchers working within the political perspective have been drawn into a more systematic analysis of the role of 'dominant coalitions' within management in structuring decision-making agendas. This is achieved through the control of underlying values and symbols that selectively legitimate certain definitions of the situation and filter out any consideration of alternative interpretations.[17] Child's[18] original formulation of the concept of dominant coalition emphasised the unobtrusive and covert control mechanisms through which shifting alliances between élite groups and middle-level experts within management shaped and framed both the agenda and process of organisational decision-making. Manipulation of ideological resources and symbolic values in such a way that the scope of the decision-making agenda and the characterisation of problems and priorities it provides are, and remain, favourable to the perceived interests of dominant groups within management has emerged as a central theme directing research and analysis.[19]

Indeed, the manipulation of dominant values and symbols by organisational and community élites – often supported by compliant professionals – has been an extremely rich seam of inquiry for those researchers attempting to ground the analysis of formal control systems in the covert processes whereby bias is mobilised in all types of work organisation.[20] As a result, the instrumental rationality assumed to be of crucial theoretical and practical importance within the technical perspective is now relocated and redefined in a new logic of analysis. This suggests that: 'under the guise and norm of rationality, power is centralised and institutionalised in organisations, and political processes are "cleared up". What is left is a system in which power and politics occur in a covert fashion, and in which there are elements of rational decision-making processes occurring simultaneously with political activity'.[21]

The development of a two-dimensional approach[22] to managerial control focused on the manipulation of ideological frameworks and the mobilisation of political bias by key groups within management has been welcomed by exponents of the critical perspective. The latter, however, advocate going one step further to the extent that they demand a much more rigorous analysis of the structural forces that determine and reproduce the forms of ideological work engaged in by many managerial élites and their expert support groups.[23]

Burawoy's[24] recent book is a prime example of the latter tendency. It focuses on the central role of management in constructing and maintaining 'particular ideological and political structures at the point of production that serve to obscure and secure surplus by organising consent on the shop floor, displacing struggles, and thus guaranteeing the reproduction of the relations *in* production'.[25] For Burawoy, the major task of management is to 'reduce or eliminate the uncertainty in the expenditure of labour while at the same time ensuring the production of profit'.[26] Thus, managerial control is deemed to be a functional necessity within capitalist work organisations because of the fundamental antagonism between capital and labour. Management control practices and structures try to resolve the opposition between these two by constructing factory regimes that provide the political and ideological apparatuses needed to regulate struggle at the point of production. These factory regimes will be crucially shaped by the state's policies in relation to the reproduction of 'labour power' and its transformation into 'labour' within the labour process.[27]

Consequently, the problem of control is the problem of realising the potential implicit in labour power into an actual labour perform- ance in such a way that surplus value and capital accumulation are secured. Managers play the key role in developing the political and ideological apparatuses through which worker co-operation and the continued generation of surplus value can be achieved. They realise this objective by concealing the underlying structural relations that determine productive activity and by legitimising the socio- economic conditions under which it is performed.[28] These political and ideological processes or mechanisms – such as bargaining systems, wage-payment systems, internal labour markets, griev- ance machinery, procedural agreements, corporate cultures and welfare provisions – provide an institutional apparatus through which managerial control can be simultaneously realised and obscured.

However, these mechanisms also exhibit contradictory pressures and outcomes. They inevitably become distorted by the negotiated compromises made necessary by the complex realities of productive activity and the constraints they impose on the operation of control systems. As a result, Burawoy concludes, the adaptive collusions or 'games' over control systems engaged in by both workers and managers establish the social stability on which continued capital accumulation depends. They also generate the political and ideo- logical constraints that shape managers' control options.[29]

The previous discussion indicates the need for a more concep- tually integrated approach to the analysis of managerial control, one that avoids the functionalist excesses characteristic of Bura- woy's study.[30] This approach – appropriately relocated within the practice perspective outlined in the previous chapter – must deal with three interrelated issues that have emerged from the above review. First, the need to distinguish analytically between different levels of control. Second, to identify the mechanisms that mediate between different levels. Third, to characterise the general proces- ses through which the connection between levels and mechanisms is reflected in managerial conduct.

The starting point for this conceptual reworking of managerial control must be Storey's contention that 'the structures and means of control are socially produced and their continued existence is therefore conditional upon managers and workers continuing to reproduce them'.[31] Thus, any particular empirical situation will reveal a 'cluster of devices, structures and practices. . . . To achieve and sustain managerial control, then, the levels and circuits of control are subject to continual experimentation'.[32] This suggests that different means and forms of managerial control practices will be operated at various levels generating an underlying instability in the overall control process as multiple devices 'oscillate, are activated, deactivated, merge and are constituted anew'.[33] While any analytical framework must drastically over-simplify the empirical complexities of particular cases, it can help to illuminate the general forms and processes revealed in individual instances.

Three levels of managerial control can be discerned in the literature[34] – corporate, organisational and workplace. Corporate-level control covers the general problem of securing the overall accommodation of workers to the long-run economic priorities of the enterprise and their implications for the broad structural constraints that will be experienced at lower levels of organisational decision-making. Organisational-level control focuses on those 'translation processes' whereby the overarching principles and priorities embodied in corporate policy are translated into operational parameters or guidelines that, in a practical manner, inform routine decision-making. Workplace-level control highlights the detailed organisation of routine work performances within the framework set by operational plans or schedules relating to items such as manning levels, production runs and line speeds.

Each of these levels relates to a specific set of mechanisms through which the problems exhibited at a particular level can be processed. Corporate-level control relates to a network of strategic allocative mechanisms dealing with the economic, political and social parameters within which productive activity will occur. The specific institutional mechanism most prominent in this area is the company boardroom and the interlocking network of relations it has with other organisations in its domain. Additional mechanisms encompassing functional specialisms located lower down the management hierarchy may also become involved.[35]

Organisational-level control relates to a set of mechanisms mediating between broad policy parameters and routine-operational detail. It entails a complex mixture of structural elements drawn from what Mintzberg calls the 'middle line', 'technostructure' and 'support staff'.[36] This includes middle-line managers with formal authority, design analysts primarily concerned with organisational standardisation and specialists located outside the operating work flow providing expert advice and support to line managers. The primary task for these mediating mechanisms is to establish and maintain a coherent link between the global policy emerging from the 'strategic apex' and the routine behaviour of the 'operating core'.

Workplace-level control relates to a network of operational mechanisms directed at securing continuity in the everyday production of surplus value in the factory and the realisation of long-term profit that it facilitates. These mechanisms relate to detailed decisions and devices concerning how immediate work tasks are to be performed according to the general specifications laid down in the operating schedules designed by middle-line personnel. First-line supervisors, foremen and junior production managers constitute the structural components that achieve routine monitoring over, and evaluation of, the 'operating core' through the deployment of a battery of formal and informal devices such as work study, overtime rosters and custom and practice.

Strategic control mechanisms depend upon those processes associated with 'synoptic rationalism'[37] – that is, formal planning procedures providing a global overview of the enterprise's future long-term development in relation to markets, products, design and organisation. The financial and technical commitments entailed in this evaluation of broad paths of future organisational development provide a crucial ideological resource that managerial élites can draw upon to legitimate certain courses of action and their deleterious impact on lower-level participants (including managers) if this is deemed necessary.

Mediate control mechanisms rely on the specialised knowledge and 'recipes for action' associated with 'logical incrementalism'[38] as a process requiring a cautious, step-by-step evolutionary development in which there is a continuing effort at building and consolidating a workable political consensus within management. The strategic objectives emerging from synoptic rationalism are modified by the tactical considerations and operational contingencies thrown up by the efforts of those managers who have to maintain sufficient organisational flexibility to facilitate an acceptable *modus vivendi* between policy constraints and production complexities.

Operational control mechanisms rest on a process of 'disjointed experimentation'[39] through which multiple control devices are tried and tested against the technical and political realities presented by workplace organisation and the shifting 'frontier of control' that it entails. A multiplicity of control devices such as rules, norms, machinery, communication networks, job design, production targets and performance reviews will be utilised, sometimes sequentially other times simultaneously, to elicit the required level of task performance from workers. A judicious mixture of coercion and persuasion will normally be relied upon by managers and supervisors to realise operational control. The balance between them will be critically dependent on the changing pattern of priorities emerging from higher levels within the management control structure.

This discussion of managerial control is summarised in diagrammatic form in Table 2.1 below:

Table 2.1   Three levels of management control

Levels	Mechanisms	Processes
Corporate	Strategic	Synoptic rationalism
Organisational	Mediate	Logical incrementalism
Workplace	Operational	Disjointed experimentation

A number of points need to be in relation to this typology and the insight it provides.

As we have already noticed, the various control levels and related mechanisms/processes are only loosely coupled together. The multiple layers and means of control that they entail fit together in an extremely untidy and disjointed manner. First, different levels of control can be in direct conflict with each other. They can overlap or they can be relatively insulated from each other in such a way that managers functioning at different levels do not have to confront the disjuncture between their particular set of control practices and those utilised at other levels.[40]

Second, managerial control is not simply imposed from above; it arises out of the struggles within and between workers and managers as they respond to the changing configuration of pressures and demands that their social situation presents.

Third, managerial control at the level of the individual firm is best viewed as an emergent phenomenon that arises out of the negotiated compromises taking place within and across all levels of the organisational hierarchy. As Edwards reflects:

> Firms will develop their practices of labour control with whatever materials they have available. They are unlikely to have explicit strategies and more likely to react to particular circumstances as best they can. Even when they have fairly clear goals they are unlikely to follow a policy which conforms to an ideal type: they will proceed according to their own needs. In particular, they are likely to use a variety of means of controlling the labour process and tying workers to the firm.[41]

Consequently, at the level of the individual enterprise and the cluster of work situations that it contains, '*the* labour process becomes a multitude of different labour processes with their own histories and organising principles'.[42] The need to relate the static typology of managerial control forms outlined above to the complexities of the dynamic social situations in which managers are actually located is obvious, and this we try to do in the section that follows.

THE DYNAMICS OF CONTROL

The need to relate forms of managerial control to the changing conditions under which they are most likely to be practised – whether at the level of a specific organisational domain, general state structures or the international system of capital accumulation – has been a recurring theme in the sociology of management. It has been most clearly expressed within the 'labour process' debate engendered by Braverman's[43] pioneering attempt to identify long-term trends in the direction of deskilling and rationalisation accompanying the development of monopoly capitalism in America since the early decades of the twentieth century.

Over the 14 years since the publication of Braverman's book, a veritable flood of publications has ensued, constituting a research tradition that takes the historical development of managerial control strategies and structures as one of its central themes.[44] In general terms, this literature has identified a long-term historical trend away from the relatively simpler forms of direct and personalised systems of control associated with internal contracting. It now embraces more complex forms of indirect and impersonal systems of control associated with the centralised bureaucratic management structures characteristic of multi-divisional business firms.[45]

This trend is seen to be closely related to the successive concentrations of capital ownership and control initiated by discontinuous merger waves at critical periods in the long-term process of capital accumulation. Thus, a more highly concentrated structure of capital ownership spanning national territorial boundaries is seen to require the centralisation of managerial control within 'a single centre of strategic calculation and control over a diversified, conglomerate and oligopoly market'.[46] This is most closely approximated in the organisational structures typical of transnational corporations. In this way, the process of capital accumulation is seen to exhibit a developmental logic that manifests itself in changes to managerial control systems in the direction of more centralised and bureaucratic forms. Capital concentration requires centralised management control systems to facilitate effective operation on an international scale.

The most influential publication within this first phase of post-Braverman research was Richard Edwards's *Contested Terrain*, published in 1979. It set the substantive historical agenda and the general analytical framework to which subsequent contributions were forced to respond.

Edwards defined a system of labour control in terms of three interrelated elements: a directive mechanism specifying the nature, timing, sequencing and precision of work tasks; an evaluative mechanism assessing and correcting work performance; and a disciplinary mechanism eliciting compliance with the capitalist's/ manager's direction of the labour process.[47] He identified three types of control as providing the co-ordination of the three elements. First, simple control, which relies on the personal interventions of gangbosses, foremen and managers. Second, technical control, which involves more formal, consciously continued controls embodied in the physical structure of the labour process. Third, bureaucratic control, which embeds control mechanisms in the social structure of the workplace, especially the institutionalisation of hierarchical power.

Edwards explains the general transformation from simple to bureaucratic control within the American economy between the middle of the nineteenth century and the second half of the twentieth century in terms of the internal logic of capitalist development and the changing organisational imperatives that it imposes on management. He allows an element of 'uneven development' in control systems and the co-existence of alternative methods in certain industrial sectors. But the underlying dynamic in his analysis suggests that greater concentration of economic resources, increased product complexity and scale of production generate the need for more elaborate forms of managerial control over workers. This is especially true in a situation where long-run industrial rationalisation is punctuated by short-run crises of intensified industrial conflict, signifying the demand for more sophisticated and effective control systems that counter worker resistance.

However, both within and without the labour process tradition there has prevailed in more recent years a growing critical reaction that has seriously undermined the logic of explanation on which earlier work has been based. It has also questioned the accuracy and generalisability of the historical interpretations it has produced.[48] This criticism has been focused on three major issues. First, the underlying determinism informing the theoretical frameworks relied upon by the first wave of labour process theorists. Second, their commitment to a linear or sequential model of historical development in managerial control systems. Third, their neglect of the inevitable contradictions between different forms of managerial control.

The functionalist logic underlying much of the work that followed Braverman's original analysis is evident in the attempt to forge a causal relationship between the changing needs of capital accumulation and the control imperatives this imposes on management. Developments in control strategies and structures are consequently reduced to an automatic and unmediated response to the economic forces at work in different phases of the accumulation process. However, more recent work has clearly indicated that 'the linkage between the logic of capital accumulation and transformation of the labour process is an indirect and varying one'.[49] The crucial mediating role played by management in interpreting the implications of macro-level developments for internal organisational control systems has assumed a central explanatory significance as the labour process has moved 'beyond the abstract statement of the differentiated functions and requirements of capital, to a consideration of how these are actually achieved, in the context of concrete mechanisms mediating between economy and work designs'.[50]

The critique of functionalism has also undermined any lingering hopes for the discovery of an 'ultimate or absolute logic in the means of control'.[51] The search for a 'magic strategy that success-fully stabilised capital/labour relations'[52] and the teleological theory of history that underpinned it[53] has been firmly rejected in favour of an approach which assumes that 'conflicting principles of labour management may be woven into the structure of the firm'.[54]

The critique of functionalism and the rejection of an evolutionary theory of control systems have encouraged a much more open recognition of 'the obvious fact that all control strategies are developing strategies which involve combinations of management practices which may involve perpetual contradiction'.[55] While general trends in the development of managerial control strategies and structures may be tentatively identified, these are now analysed and interpreted within a theoretical context that highlights the contradictory requirements and outcomes that these trends inevit-ably produce. As Hyman reflects:

> Strategic choice exists, not because of the weaknesses of structural determinations, but because these determinations are themselves contradictory. . . . For individual capitals – as for capital in general – there is no 'one best way' of managing these contradictions, only different routes to partial failure. It is on this basis that managerial strategy can best be concep-tualized: as the programmatic choice among alternatives, none of which can prove satisfactory.[56]

It is with this proposition in mind that we can now deploy the typology constructed in the previous section to illuminate whatever long-term trends in management control strategies and structures have provisionally emerged from more recent research.

Broadly, we can discern two interpretations of long-term trends in managerial control strategies and structures. First, those research-ers who have identified a long-term trend in the direction of more integrated control systems, where the levels, processes and mechanisms outlined in the previous section are realigned to pro-duce a much more tightly coupled hierarchy of managerial control.[57] Second, those researchers who offer an alternative inter-pretation, which points in the direction of more internally differ-entiated control systems that remain relatively autonomous from each other.[58]

The first group identifies a convergence between more advanced integrated control systems developed at corporate level – particularly the extension of centralised management information and budgetary control systems – and computer-based production control systems facilitated by the introduction of microelectronic technology at the workplace level. Thus, Storey suggests that 'the availability of potentially more powerful control devices, and the intensification of the competition to secure surplus value, seems likely to ensure that the multiple levels and circuits of control explored in this paper will decline in importance and integration will increase'.[59]

Burawoy expresses, in much more dramatic terms, this tighter integration of corporate, organisational and workplace control systems under the driving force exerted by intensified capitalist competition on an international scale:

> The rise of hegemonic regimes, tying the interests of the workers to the fortunes of their employers, embodying working class power in factory rather than state apparatuses, and the reinforcement of individualism has left workers defenceless against the recent challenges of capital. . . . The new despotism is founded on the basis of the hegemonic regime it is replacing. It is in fact a hegemonic despotism. The interests of capital and labour continue to be concretely co-ordinated, but where labour used to be *granted* concessions on the basis of the expansion of profits, it now *makes* concessions on the basis of the relative profitability of one capitalist vis-a-vis another. . . . The new despotism is the 'rational' tyranny of capital mobility over the *collective* worker . . . there are signs that in all advanced capitalist societies hegemonic regimes are developing a despotic face . . . the underlying dynamics, the changing international division of labour and capital mobility, are leading toward . . . hegemonic despotism.[60]

This suggests that a sophisticated combination of rational control techniques and ideologically motivated devices (such as quality circles, briefing groups, works councils and participation schemes), which is aimed at mobilising worker consent to increased productivity, has emerged as the dominant control structure under advanced capitalism. Lower-level operating units within the company may be allowed some degree of discretion. Yet, 'hegemonic despotism' signifies the move to a form of integrated control in which middle- and lower-level managers are strictly conditioned by the strategic economic and political imperatives imposed by corporate directors and senior managers as constituent members of the structure of intercorporate networks that dominates advanced capitalist economies.[61]

The second group of researchers emphasises the continued differentiation, not to say fragmentation, of control strategies and structures both within and between business corporations. Child maintains that:

> Differentiated employment policies will therefore be evident at the level of a single plant, such that particularly valued groups may be upgraded and encouraged to acquire new skills while others are possibly degraded, eliminated or placed on limited contracts. In short, similarities and differences in managerial strategies need to be analysed at various system levels.[62]

This argument is supported by Nichols[63] in a review of the major developments that have occurred in management control strategies and structures in Britain since the latter half of the 1970s. His review clearly identifies a trend towards greater flexibility[64] in managerial control systems based on a form of work organisation that differentiates between core and peripheral units or work groups and requires a shift towards the casualisation of labour located in the latter category. These developments have also initiated more extensive internal segmentation within management control practices such that core workers enjoy a level of employment security, status and remuneration far above that of peripheral workers. The former are also subjected to various forms of ideological socialisation deemed to be unnecessary for the latter.[65]

Francis[66] concludes his analysis of the control implications of new technology by suggesting that a general trend has begun away from hierarchical systems to more flexible market-based systems. However, the extensiveness of this development will depend crucially on the influence of conditions prevailing in product and labour markets, corporate histories and cultures, and the distribution of bargaining powers and skills among organisational stakeholders.

Hyman distils and synthesises the general implications of the overall findings of this second group of researchers when he concludes that:

the obstacles to integration are considerable; and even where coherent labour control strategies can be discerned, their diversity is likely to be far greater than is recognised in the typologies proposed by recent writers. . . . Variation is reinforced by the problematics of internal management cohesion and control. . . . Underlying both the potential lack of integration between levels of intervention and the impact of internal management division is the underlying contradiction involved in capitalist control over labour; and it is this, in turn, which creates a potential for worker initiative in ways which further adapt and qualify the strategies of management.[67]

This indicates that we need an approach to the analysis of managerial control systems that is sensitive to the breaks and ruptures that inevitably occur between corporate strategies and their actual implementation in the organisation of the labour process and at the level of work task design.[68] The mediating role performed by middle managers, work organisation designers and workers in translating general objectives and imperatives into operational systems also needs to be explored.[69]

However, before we can proceed to ground the analysis of control forms more fully in the process of managerial work, we need to look more closely at the concept of contradiction that has emerged as a key consideration throughout this discussion.

THE CONTRADICTIONS OF CONTROL

The apparent divergence between the integration and differentiation theses of long-run trends in managerial control systems may become less dramatic once we take the inevitable contradictions of managerial strategy more fully into account. Indeed, conterminous development of control systems in the direction of a mixed model, consisting of a range of managerial practices that simultaneously cope with old control problems and generate new ones, is to be expected if the concept of contradiction is given the attention it requires.

Zeitlin[70] argues that management's attempt to control recalcitrant labour will always be limited by the capacity of the latter to impose some degree of constraint on the changes the former will try to implement under intensified market competition.

> If we begin our analysis from the bottom up, from the perspective of the enterprise rather than that of society as a whole, it becomes apparent that some degree of job control is an inevitable result of the internal contradictions of any possible managerial strategy. Even if we assume, therefore, that managers always seek to control a recalcitrant labour force, the inadequacies of the strategies available to them make this goal unattainable in practice. . . . Over the long-term, therefore, management must bargain for the voluntary co-operation of its workers: and as a result, it is forced to accept some formal or informal limitations on its authority in the workplace. The resulting proliferation of work rules and bargaining procedures in turn defines the contours of that antagonistic co-operation which is the normal relationship between workers and employers in capitalist societies.[71]

He develops this point through a more detailed consideration of the distinction Friedman[72] makes between 'direct control' and 'responsible autonomy' as alternative labour control strategies available to management in different economic, technological and social circumstances. Direct control aims to minimise management's dependence on labour by reducing as far as possible the initiative and skill required for task performance. This is attempted through the implementation of a tightly structured and integrated system of workplace control, which is continually monitored and directed by higher-level mechanisms within the company. Responsible autonomy concedes a measure of discretion and influence to workers in task performance within the labour process. But it seeks to channel its use in accordance with managerial objectives by deploying a much more internally differentiated set of control mechanisms in which the need for ideological indoctrination is regarded as central.

Yet, neither of these strategies, Zeitlin contends, 'can be pursued consistently to the exclusion of the other, and it is from the resulting gap in managerial authority that opportunities for job control emerge'.[73] This is so to the extent that neither strategy frees management from the need to get some level of willing co-operation from its workforce, and both generate novel control problems stemming directly from the practices they entail.

Management's move towards a more direct and integrated control strategy makes the operation of the labour process and the continuation of capital accumulation more problematic because it renders the organisation more vulnerable to the disruptive action of strategically located work groups.[74] Development in the direction of responsible autonomy entails the risk of considerable internal fragmentation in managerial control systems, which in turn makes it difficult to ensure that workers' initiatives are taken in line with policy parameters issuing from the corporate level. Each control strategy generates its own internal problems in the very process of dealing with the difficulties it was designed to solve. These strategies also reveal the considerable scope for bargaining and collusion at all levels of the managerial control hierarchy. This inevitably distorts the ideal relationship anticipated between planning, implementation and outcomes within the overall control process.

Zeitlin's analysis is reinforced by other recent contributors to the 'control debate' such as Watson,[75] Edwards[76] and Hyman.[77] Watson finds that management control strategies are forced to mediate between the simultaneous need for industrial discipline, imposed by the structure of industrial capitalism, and the demand for freedom and autonomy, implied in the notion of formally free labour. The tensions this creates are most strongly felt, he suggests, by personnel specialists, who are 'involved directly in the utilising and controlling of people as labour resources and also playing a significant part in coming to terms with the conflicts and instabilities following from such efforts'.[78]

Edwards maintains that management will attempt to secure worker compliance through a complex range of employment policies and practices that destroys any aspiration towards fully integrated control systems functioning within one homogeneous mode of control.[79] These employment control strategies co-exist in a state of mutual tension insofar as they are directed at securing the deployment of workers' productive capacities within a production process based on a relationship of structured antagonism between dominant and subordinate groups. Management control mechanisms and structures emerge out of a process of social conflict that crystallises around issues concerned with the way in which the labour process is organised. As such:

'Control', need not, then, be seen as a matter of deliberate managerial policy. A system or a structure of control can contain a variety of elements which have been assembled as the result of particular responses to particular problems. Yet such a system or structure has real consequences for the way in which work is perceived and for what actions are possible. It is not simply imposed from above, for it reflects previous struggles; yet it constrains behaviour on the part of managers as well as workers.[80]

Hyman's analysis of recent trends in managerial control strategies and structures provides a synthesis of these views in that it focuses analytical attention upon the contradictory requirements of labour management in advanced capitalist societies:

the function of labour control involves *both* the direction, surveillance and discipline of subordinates whose enthusiastic commitment to corporate objectives cannot be taken for granted; and the mobilisation of the discretion, initiative and diligence which coercive supervision, far from guaranteeing, is likely to destroy. . . . Shifting fashions in labour management stem from this inherent contradiction: solutions to the problem of discipline aggravate the problem of consent and vice versa. . . . Employers require workers to be both dependable and disposable . . . contradictory pressures within capitalism help explain the restless but fruitless search for managerial panaceas.[81]

Hyman cautions against any interpretations that conflate different levels of analysis and assume that management control strategies can be simply read off from the structural imperatives imposed by the logic of capitalist accumulation. Instead, he offers an assessment that lays overwhelming emphasis upon the partial autonomy of distinctive control levels and processes, to say nothing of the contradictory pressures they exert on management. In this situation, a mixture of pragmatism, opportunism and incrementalism is often the most sensible basis on which labour management control strategies should be designed and implemented. Changes to the balance of power both within and between management and labour can lead to the development of somewhat more aggressive policies of labour management control. Yet, Hyman sees little evidence for the trend towards the hegemonic despotism identified by Burawoy.

Indeed, Hyman highlights the crucial importance of internal managerial politics in shaping labour control strategies and practices:

> Principles and policies of labour control enunciated at the top may thus be diluted and transmuted further down the managerial hierarchy in irregular accommodations with subordinate employees . . . the policies formally adopted by top management will be effective in practice only if guaranteed through the mechanisms of restrictions, control and direction that they impose on line management.[82]

Consequently, variations in control systems arising from the wider socio-economic environment in which management operates are reinforced by intra-managerial bargaining and micro-political struggles, which require negotiated control strategies in practice. As Hyman indicates: 'Variation is reinforced by the problematics of internal management cohesion and control'.[83]

Sociological research on management control strategies has produced a wealth of case study material, which illustrates the significance of 'contradiction' for an understanding of the realities of managerial practice. Selected examples of this material are reviewed in the following section in order to provide a more grounded appreciation of the practical control dilemmas that managers confront in their struggles to organise productive activity.

CONTROL AS A PRACTICAL DILEMMA

Much of the previous discussion of managerial control strategies and structures can be analytically captured in Gidden's concept of the 'dialectic of control':

> Power relations in social systems can be regarded as relations of autonomy and dependence; but no matter how imbalanced they may be in terms of power, actors in subordinate positions are never wholly dependent and are often very adept at converting whatever resources they possess into some degree of control over the conditions of reproduction of the system.

In all social systems there is a dialectic of control, such that
there are normally continually shifting balances of resources
altering the overall distribution of power.[84]

Any labour control strategy mobilised by management will have
some potential for increasing – rather than decreasing – the control
exercised by subordinate groups within the organisation. Management control strategies will inevitably produce perverse consequences insofar as they present opportunities for workers (or
lower-level managers) to reduce their dependence on management
and to widen their operational autonomy. If these opportunities are
exploited,[85] it is likely that conflict will ensue as a result of the power
struggles that will cohere around sources of potential control made
available by managerial initiatives aimed at removing them. The
emergence of these alternative sources of subordinate control are
likely to lead to a redoubling of managerial efforts to eradicate
them, which, in turn, will produce new opportunities for subordinates to exploit the control potential that the latter provide. In this
sense, the process of managerial control is best understood as a set
of loosely connected practices and mechanisms that will inevitably
generate unintended consequences in the very act of providing
solutions to recognised problems.

The best example of the dialectic of managerial control within the
case study literature is to be found in that series of empirical case
studies on the 'dynamics of bureaucracy' published between the late
1940s and mid-1960s.[86] These have been followed by a succession of
research monographs and papers that provide further insight into
the processes whereby managers are forced to cope with the conflicting pressures reproduced by their own control strategies and
practices.[87] Three examples will be selected from this body of
literature and briefly discussed in relation to the practical insight
they provide into the dialectic of managerial control.

Gouldner's study[88] focuses upon the development of a more
centralised bureaucratic control system in an industrial organisation
over a three-year period between 1948 and 1951. He analyses this
shift away from a more decentralised, flexible and personal form of
managerial control – which he labels the indulgency pattern – in
relation to the dramatic socio-economic changes that occurred in
the local community and specific industrial sectors over this period.
This environmental context of a declining rural community under-

going economic rationalisation, and an industrial sector characterised by increased competition in its product market, encouraged management to implement a more formalised control system based on an economistic ideology. This treated workers as factors of production to be used to maximum economic benefit with little or no regard for their status as moral agents. The ethical commitments and moral claims recognised under the paternalistic ideology supporting the indulgency patterns were swept away by a control system and an ideology that redefined the employment relationship in narrow economic terms shorn of any moral considerations.

The imposition of bureaucratic control eventually resulted in a wildcat strike in April 1950, which was finally settled after several weeks of difficult negotiation between the company and the union in the late spring of 1950. The collective agreement that settled the strike directly reinforced the bureaucratisation of labour–management relations that had begun in 1949. It intensified a centralisation of decision-making processes in both management and union hierarchies, extended the range and sophistication of formal control mechanisms, and strengthened an economistic ideology as a basis for future organisational involvement.

Nevertheless, the implementation of bureaucratic control generated its own tensions and conflicts, which eventually presented major problems for successive generations of managers. A more formalised bureaucratic control regime and a supporting economistic ideology provided the conditions in which workers could more effectively challenge the exercise of managerial prerogative in the future. The underlying stability and flexibility provided by the indulgency pattern had been virtually destroyed. It had been replaced by a more transient and fragile set of relationships that proved extremely brittle when new waves of organisational rationalisation became necessary. The bureaucratisation of managerial control systems, and the rationalisation of practices and ideology that it entailed, had unintentionally produced a workforce that was now much better prepared to engage in industrial action in pursuit of rational economic objectives. The latent realities of power and control underlying the indulgency pattern had been fully exposed to provide a very different organisational and ideological setting in which future generations of managers would be forced to operate.

Krieger analyses the implementation of a more centralised system of bureaucratic management control within the National Coal

Board (now British Coal) as represented in the development of a national wages policy dovetailed with systematic manpower planning. In this way, NCB management intended 'to increase control, not only over earnings, but over the determination of task, team composition, and the process of production and turnover of the face'.[89] However, moves in this direction had such a destabilising impact on the internal political economy of the coal industry that industrial conflict was intensified, productivity levels were substantially reduced, and national unity within the National Union of Mineworkers reached a level that would eventually defeat a government (in the general election of 1974).

Krieger examines these unforeseen consequences in terms of the internal contradictions of a strategy of centralised bureaucratic control and their interaction with the changing contours of capitalist economic development as they impinge on State policy:

> Management reasoned rightly and planned well but were not equipped to understand the full range of consequences which followed from the simple, uniform, national time-based wage structure. A centralising policy was torn apart by the centrifugal pressures of a regionally distinctive industry. A policy which was designed thoughtfully to reward a simply instrumental reaction – co-operation in return for a guaranteed wage – succumbed before the complex meanings attached to it by workers who had long been influenced by labouring relations which occasioned responses that management had not foreseen. Accordingly, a policy designed to rationalise and harmonise a basic industry with unusual economic and political centrality seemed instead to undermine capitalism.[90]

The failure of bureaucratic centralism, Krieger concludes, is not a failure of the logic of the policy-making and implementing process, but one that must be traced to the 'dialectic of control which attends centralised bureaucratic administration'.[91] Instead of reducing power struggles over production decisions – at the level of the individual colliery, regional organisation or national headquarters – and freeing management from constant bargaining and bickering, the move to a national day-wage structure planned and controlled by a centralised bureaucracy exacerbated underlying tensions. It also created novel sources of strain and conflict that eventually overwhelmed management. Centralised bureaucratic management reshaped a fluid struggle for control at all levels of the NCB's organisational hierarchy in a direction that eventually resulted in the administrative unravelling of the wages policy it had initiated. In particular, it attempted to graft on to the mining labour process and industrial relations system a structure of bureaucratic administration that would reduce workers' autonomy by enmeshing them within a tight framework of formalised rules and surveillance devices. In the event, the National Union of Mineworkers turned this system to their own advantage by undermining the new supervisory and manning practices it entailed. This, in turn, eventually produced a form of industrial conflict in which a highly differentiated and regionalised labour force exhibited a degree of national unity and co-ordination in industrial action that directly contrasted with the extremely fragmented and disjointed pattern typical of the earlier regime of decentralised managerial control.

Batstone, Ferner and Terry[92] trace the development of a more flexible and decentralised labour relations strategy in the Post Office in response to the external pressure for greater commercial realism in an institution previously dominated by an ideology of corporate paternalism and bureaucratic centralism. However, implementation of the specific components of this decentralised control strategy – more flexible grading structures, weakening of the internal labour market, developing more efficient and flexible forms of work organisation, directly linking pay and performance, reforming the system of joint regulation – created deep-seated tensions both within the management and trade union structures as well as between them. In both the postal and telecommunications sectors of the Post Office there was a basic split within management between the traditionalists, who wished to preserve the best of the established labour relations system, and the commercialists (politically stronger in telecommunications), who were determined to break the constraints imposed by the old consensus and to reassert control over labour. The traditionalists advocated an incremental change strategy maintaining the stability and order facilitated by established structures; the commercialists pressed for a much more aggressive labour relations strategy in which more decentralised and targeted control mechanisms were implemented to undermine corporatist arrangements.

The latter strategy proved much more influential within telecommunications, because of its relative economic and technological significance, and its attractiveness to private financial interests. Its management was also much more receptive to a commercial view of labour relations than its counterpart in the postal side of the business, which remained ideologically and organisationally committed to a quasi-civil service conception of its role. In addition, the pressure exerted by a government determined to increase public sector efficiency and to modernise its services in a dynamic market was another crucial factor encouraging fuller acceptance of a flexible, decentralised and market-based labour relations strategy.

Nevertheless, the move towards a commercial labour relations strategy in telecommunications faced severe implementation problems. Growing dissatisfaction and insecurity on the part of the trade unions eventually led to the outbreak of industrial conflict, which threatened organisational change in the direction of a market-oriented philosophy. As a result, management were eventually forced to return to selected elements of a strategy of bureaucratic centralism that had officially been rejected as an acceptable basis on which to proceed.

This was particularly true in relation to management's attempts to reduce the significance of national level agreements and to regain and retain control over the details of work organisation at local level. A more planned and aggressive bargaining strategy, emphasising the material and career gains to be realised from the removal of traditional reward structures and their replacement by achievement-related rewards, was the central means chosen to achieve this objective. However, the destabilising impact of industrial conflict:

> led inevitably to a reliance in practice on seasoned managers versed in the arts of compromise and conflict avoidance, and capable of manipulating their long-standing relations of mutual trust with union leaders in order to solve problems. Thus the pragmatic style of industrial relations continually reasserted itself. This sometimes led to ad hoc solutions to problems which offended the desires for a new firm and coherent line.[93]

The tension between a logic of commercialism and modernisation, which demanded the implementation of a revolutionary labour relations strategy reasserting control at workplace level, and a traditionalist ideology, which stressed the primacy of corporate order and stability, became even more acute as the pressure for privatisation intensified. This made it even harder for management to get control over labour and to keep its co-operation when, given the political climate, the argument for a new moral basis for consensus was unlikely to win much sympathy.

Each of these case studies illustrates the contradictory implications of alternative control strategies and the need for management to cope with the conflicting pressures they generate. They reveal also the need for a form of sociological analysis that is sensitive to the complexities of strategy formulation and implementation in a dynamic socio-economic context always likely to undermine the internal logic of a preferred strategy. The role of micro-political processes within management in interpreting and assessing the impact of alternative control strategies also emerges as a central theme to be pursued in the next chapter.

CONCLUSION

This chapter has reviewed the contribution sociological research and analysis have made to a better understanding of managerial control strategies and structures. The major theme it has revealed is the contradictory nature of the control process and the overriding need to relate changing managerial strategies to the dynamic social contexts in which they are implemented. It has also reinforced the argument that long-term developments in control strategies and structures must be grounded in a more sophisticated understanding of the complexities of the organisational work in which managers are necessarily engaged.

The latter theme is discussed more fully in the next chapter.

REFERENCES

1. For a more detailed elaboration of this view see Lowe, T. and Machin, L.J., *New Perspectives in Management and Control* (Macmillan, London, 1983).
2. For an empirical case study that effectively illustrates this point see Pettigrew, A., *The Politics of Organisational Decision-Making* (Tavistock, London, 1973).
3. For a further development of the concept of 'structured antagonism'

and its significance for analysing forms of industrial conflict within the workplace see Edwards, P.K., *Conflict at Work* (Basil Blackwell, Oxford, 1986).

4. On this point see Harris, C.C., *Fundamental Concepts and the Sociological Enterprise* (Allen and Unwin, London, 1980).

5. For a recent review of the literature that clearly establishes this point see Hyman, R., 'Strategy or Structure?: Capital, Labour and Control', *Work, Employment and Society* vol. 1, No. 1, (1987) pp. 25–55.

6. This concept is taken from Thompson, J.D., *Organisations in Action* (McGraw-Hill, New York, 1967).

7. Woodward, J., *Industrial Organisation: Behaviour and Control* (Oxford University Press, London, 1970).

8. Etzioni, A., *A Comparative Analysis of Complex Organisations* (Free Press, New York, 2nd edition, 1975).

9. Thompson, J.D., op. cit., (1967).

10. This classification is taken from Parsons, T., *Structure and Process in Modern Societies* (Free Press, New York, 1960).

11. Thompson, J.D., op. cit., (1967), p. 12.

12. Lowe, T. and Machin, L.J., op. cit., (1983).

13. On this point see Hopper, T.M. and Berry, A.J., 'Organisational Design and Management Control' in Lowe, T. and Machin, L.J., op. cit., (1983), pp. 97–117.

14. Dalton, M., *Men Who Manage* (John Wiley and Son, New York, 1959).

15. Burns, T., *The BBC* (Macmillan, London, 1977).

16. Pettigrew, A., op. cit., (1973).

17. For recent examples of organisational analysis texts that focus on this point see Legge, K., *Power, Innovation and Problem-Solving in Personnel Management* (McGraw-Hill, London, 1978); Perrow, C., *Complex Organisations: A Critical Essay* (Scott Foresman, Dallas, 2nd edition, 1976); Dawson, S., *Analysing Organisations* (Macmillan, London, 1986).

18. Child, J., 'Organisational Structure, Environment and Performance: The Role of Strategic Choice', *Sociology* vol. 6, No. 1, (1972), pp. 234–57.

19. For two recent examples see Pfeffer, J., *Power in Organisations* (Pitman, Massachusetts, 1981) and Morgan, G., *Images of Organisation* (Sage, California, 1986).

20. For examples of this research see Bachrach, P. and Baratz, M.S., *Power and Poverty* (Oxford University Press, London, 1971); Crenson, M.A., *The Un-Politics of Air Pollution: A Study of Non-Decision-Making in the Cities* (John Hopkins Press, Baltimore, 1971).

21. Pfeffer, J., op. cit., (1981), p. 345.

22. There is an obvious parallel here with Lukes's two-dimensional view of power elaborated in Lukes, S., *Power: A Radical View* (Macmillan, London, 1974).

23. As conducted, for example, in Daudi, P., *The Discourse of Power in Managerial Praxis* (Basil Blackwell, Oxford, 1986).

24. Burawoy, M., *The Politics of Production* (Verso, London, 1985).
25. Ibid., p. 49.
26. Ibid., p. 27.
27. Burawoy suggests that the link between state apparatus and factory regime is one in which the former underwrites and guarantees the latter through various regulatory mechanisms and strategies. For a more detailed elaboration of this point see Burawoy, M., op. cit., (1985), pp. 11–19.
28. This argument is developed in greater detail in Burawoy, M., op. cit., (1985), pp. 35–40.
29. This theme is discussed in greater detail in Chapter five.
30. The functionalist determinism informing Burawoy's analysis is analysed further in Reed, M., 'Labour Process Theory and the Sociology of Management', mimeograph, University College, Cardiff, 1985.
31. Storey, J., 'The Means of Management Control', *Sociology*, vol. 19, No. 2, (1985a), pp. 193–211.
32. Ibid., pp. 198–9.
33. Ibid., p. 207.
34. For recent examples that illustrate this point see Storey, J., 'Management Control as a Bridging Concept', *Journal of Management Studies*, vol. 22, No. 3, (1985b), pp. 269–91; Clegg, S., Boreham, P. and Dow, G., *Class Politics and the Economy* (Routledge and Kegan Paul, London, 1986).
35. For two studies that illustrate this point see Pahl, R.E. and Winkler, J.T., 'The Economic Elite: Theory and Practice', in Stanworth, P. and Giddens, A. (eds.), *Elites and Power in British Society* (Cambridge University Press, Cambridge, 1974) and Pettigrew, A., *The Awakening Giant: Continuity and Change in ICI* (Basil Blackwell, Oxford, 1985).
36. Mintzberg, H., *The Structuring of Organisations* (Prentice-Hall, Englewood Cliffs, N.J., 1979).
37. For a more detailed analysis of this concept and the related concept of global intelligence see Simon, H., *The New Science of Management Decision-Making* (Prentice-Hall, Englewood Cliffs, N.J., rev. edition, 1977) and Ansoff, H.I., *Corporate Strategy* (McGraw-Hill, New York, 1965).
38. This concept is taken from Quinn, M., *Strategies for Change: Logical Incrementalism* (Irwin, Illinois, 1980).
39. This is an adaptation of Lindblom's concept of disjointed incrementalism, as outlined in Lindblom, C.E., 'The Science of Muddling Through', *Public Administration Review*, vol. 19, (1959), pp. 79–88.
40. For empirical illustrations of this point see Storey, J., op. cit., (1985a).
41. Edwards, P.K., op. cit., (1986), p. 41.
42. Ibid., p. 78.
43. Braverman, H., *Labour and Monopoly Capital* (Monthly Review Press, New York, 1974).
44. Friedman, A.L., *Industry and Labour* (Macmillan, London, 1977); Edwards, R., *Contested Terrain* (Heinemann, London, 1979); Claw-

son, D., *Bureaucracy and the Labour Process* (Monthly Review Press, New York, 1980); Littler, C.R., *The Development of the Labour Process in Capitalist Societies* (Heinemann, London, 1982); Gordon, D., Edwards, R. and Reich, F., *Segmented Work, Divided Workers* (Cambridge University Press, Cambridge, 1982); Zimblast, A. (ed.), *Case Studies on the Labour Process* (Monthly Review Press, New York, 1979); Wood, S. (ed.), *The Degradation of Work?* (Hutchinson, London, 1982); Montgomery, D. (ed.), *Workers' Control in America* (Cambridge University Press, Cambridge, 1980).

45. For an excellent review of this long-term trend see Clegg, S., Boreham, P. and Dow, G., op. cit., (1986), pp. 92–105.

46. Ibid., p. 102. For a useful, if somewhat staid, review of the range of control systems and practices utilised by transnational corporations see Brooke, M.Z. and Remners, H.L., *The Strategy of Multinational Enterprise* (Pitman, London, 2nd edition, 1978).

47. Edwards, R., op. cit., (1979), p. 18. For an elaboration of this conceptual framework for analysing labour control systems/strategies see Littler, C.R. and Salaman, G., *Class at Work* (Batsford, London, 1984).

48. For two recent reviews that relate to this point see Thompson, P., *The Nature of Work* (Macmillan, London, 1983) and Wood, S., 'Work Organisation' in Deam, R. and Salaman, G. (eds.), *Work Culture and Society* (Open University Press, Milton Keynes, 1985), pp. 77–101.

49. Littler, C.R., op. cit., (1982), p. 34.

50. Salaman, G., 'Managing the Frontier of Control', in Giddens, A. and Mackenzie, G., (eds.), *Social Class and the Division of Labour* (Cambridge University Press, Cambridge, 1982), pp. 46–62 (p. 62).

51. Storey, J., op. cit., (1985a), p. 1971.

52. Littler, C.R. and Salaman, G., 'Bravermania and Beyond: Recent Theories of the Labour Process', *Sociology*, vol. 16, No. 2, (1982), pp. 251–69 (p. 264).

53. The extent to which a teleological view of history may be said to underpin labour process analysis of managerial control strategies and structures is assessed in Zeitlin, J., 'Shop Floor Bargaining and the State: A Contradictory Relationship', in Tolliday, S. and Zeitlin, J. (eds.), *Shop Floor Bargaining and the State: Historical and Comparative Perspectives* (Cambridge University Press, Cambridge, 1985), pp. 1–45 and Friedman, A.L., 'The Means of Management Control and Labour Process Theory: A Critical Note on Storey', *Sociology*, vol. 21, No. 2, (1987), pp. 287–94.

54. Rose, M. and Jones, B., 'Managerial Strategy and Trade Union Responses in Work Re-organisation Schemes at Establishment Level', in Knights, D., Willmott, H. and Collinson, D. (eds.), *Job Redesign: Critical Perspectives on the Labour Process* (Gower, Aldershot, 1985), pp. 81–106.

55. Littler, C.R. and Salaman, G., op. cit., (1982), p. 264.

56. Hyman, R., op. cit., (1987), p. 30.

57. Examples of this view are to be found in Edwards, R., op. cit., (1979);

Storey, J., op. cit., (1985a); Burawoy, M., op. cit., (1985); Clegg, S., Boreham, P. and Dow, G., op. cit., (1986); and Scott, J., *Corporations, Classes and Capitalism* (Hutchinson, London, 2nd edition, 1985).

58. Examples of this view occur in Gospel, H., 'The Development of Management Organisation in Industrial Relations: A Historical Perspective', in Thurley, K. and Wood, S. (eds.), *Industrial Relations and Management Strategy* (Cambridge University Press, Cambridge, 1983), pp. 91–110; Child, J., 'Managerial Strategies, New Technology and the Labour Process', in Knights, D., Willmott, H. and Collinson, D., op. cit., (1985), pp. 107–41; Francis, A., *New Technology at Work* (Oxford University Press, Oxford, 1986); Nichols, T., *The British Worker Question* (Routledge and Kegan Paul, London, 1986); Starkey, K. and McKinlay, A., 'Changing Work Organisation in the 1980's', Work Organisation Research Centre, Aston University, 1987, mimeograph.

59. Storey, J., op. cit., (1985a), p. 207.

60. Burawoy, M., op. cit., (1985), pp. 150–2.

61. On this point see Scott, J., op. cit., (1985), pp. 180–93.

62. Child, J., in Knights, Willmott and Collinson (eds.), op. cit., (1985), p. 134.

63. Nichols, T., op. cit., (1986).

64. The concept of flexible specialisation and its implications *for* management are discussed in greater detail in Chapter six.

65. The parallel with Friedman's distinction between 'responsible autonomy' and 'direct control' as alternative strategies is obvious here. So is Child's distinction between 'cultural control' and 'bureaucratic control', insofar as it contrasts a strategy based on normative indoctrination and limited autonomy with one based on formalisation and standardisation as mechanisms for securing compliance. On the latter point see Child, J., *Organisation: A Guide to Problems and Practice* (Harper and Row, London, 2nd edition, 1984), pp. 157–65.

66. Francis, A., op. cit., (1986).

67. Hyman, R., op. cit., (1987), pp. 48–9.

68. For a further development of this point see Child, J., in Knights, Willmott and Collinson (eds.), op. cit., (1985), pp. 107–12.

69. A case study that perceptively illustrates this point is Hopper, T., Cooper, D., Lowe, T., Capps, T. and Mouritsen, J., 'Management Control and Worker Resistance in the National Coal Board: Financial Controls in the Labour Process', in Knights, D. and Willmott, H. (eds.), *Managing the Labour Process* (Gower, Aldershot, 1986), pp. 109–41.

70. Zeitlin, J., op. cit., (1985).

71. Ibid., pp. 13–15.

72. Friedman, A., op. cit.

73. Zeitlin, J., op. cit., (1985), p. 14.

74. This insight is explored to great effect in Crozier, M., *The Bureaucratic Phenomenon* (University of Chicago Press, Chicago, 1964).

75. Watson, T.J., *Management, Organisation and Employment Strategy* (Routledge and Kegan Paul, London, 1986).
76. Edwards, P.K., op. cit., (1986).
77. Hyman, R., op. cit., (1987).
78. Watson, T., 'Towards a General Theory of Personnel and Industrial Relations Management', *Trent Business School, Occasional Paper Series*, No. 2, (1983), p. 24.
79. Edwards, P.K., op. cit., (1986), pp. 154–5.
80. Ibid., p. 80.
81. Hyman, R., op. cit., (1987), pp. 41–3.
82. Ibid., p. 41.
83. Ibid., p. 49.
84. Giddens, A., 'Power, the Dialetic of Control and Class Structuration', in Giddens, A. and Mackenzie, G., op. cit., (1982), pp. 29–45 (p. 32). Giddens has developed this idea further in Giddens, A., *The Constitution of Society* (Polity Press, Cambridge, 1984).
85. The contingent factors relating to this issue are examined further in Chapter four.
86. For a detailed discussion and re-evaluation of this body of literature see Reed, M., *Redirections in Organisational Analysis* (Tavistock, London, 1985).
87. For a pioneering example of research on this topic see Burns, T. and Stalker, G.M., *The Management of Innovation* (Tavistock, London, 1961).
88. Gouldner, A., *Patterns of Industrial Bureaucracy* (Free Press, New York, 1954a) and *Wildcat Strike* (Antioch Press, New York, 1954b).
89. Krieger, J., *Undermining Capitalism: State Ownership and the Dialectic of Control in the British Coal Industry* (Pluto Press, London, 1984), p. 16.
90. Ibid., p. 267.
91. Ibid., p. 34.
92. Batstone, E., Ferner, A. and Terry, M., *Consent and Efficiency: Labour Relations and Management Strategy in the State Enterprise* (Basil Blackwell, Oxford, 1984).
93. Ibid., p. 160.

3

MANAGERIAL WORK

INTRODUCTION

The previous chapters have outlined the major theoretical perspectives that have been developed within the sociology of management. They have explored the application of these perspectives to the central substantive theme emerging from sociological analysis of management organisation and behaviour – that is, the process of managerial control.

This chapter focuses upon the nature of managerial work within the theoretical and substantive parameters set by the previous chapters. It carries out this task in a number of respects. First, it reviews the various explanations that have been offered for the historical development of modern management – both as a unique organisational form and as a distinctive ideological world view. Second, it considers the various conceptions of managerial work that have evolved within sociological analysis since the inception of the corporate system in western industrialised societies during the early years of the twentieth century. Third, it assesses the implications of empirical research on the three major levels of management that have crystallised within contemporary corporate hierarchies. These are made up of the élite group of directors and senior managers; the middle strata of line managers and technical experts that implement corporate policy; and the cadre of first-line supervisors and foremen, who are the superintendents of production. A concluding section evaluates the general contribution sociological analysis has made to our understanding of the nature of managerial work.

THE GENESIS OF MODERN MANAGEMENT[1]

Three general explanatory frameworks have been deployed to provide coherent and systematic accounts of the development of complex managerial hierarchies in western industrialised societies from the latter half of the nineteenth century onwards.

First, the framework that explains the genesis of modern management in terms of the relative technical efficiency and profitability of such an organisational form over alternative methods of economic co-ordination and allocation such as the market.[2] Second, those writers who have constructed an explanation of managerial development that concentrates on the economic, political and social power exercised by managerial élites.[3] Third, an explanatory logic that focuses upon the class interests served by managerial organisation in capitalist systems.[4] We shall consider each of these[5] in turn, before moving on to examine the ideological correlates of these organisational developments.

The view that modern managerial hierarchies developed as a result of their comparative technical efficiency in co-ordinating large-scale productive activity for private profit is eloquently summarised below:

> The rapid growth of the multiunit modern business firm in some industrial sectors suggests that the hierarchical structure proved more efficient than market mechanisms . . . in co-ordinating the activities of production and distribution units in those sectors. The hierarchical co-ordination of units within the modern business firm relies on the consolidation of ownership and also, more significantly, on the development of sophisticated control instruments for the various units it co-ordinates and monitors. The firm's efficiency in allocating such funds and personnel over its distribution and production units influences its competitive advantage over other institutional arrangements. The functions of the modern firm, then, are co-ordination, monitoring and the allocation of resources. It is in carrying out these crucial functions in combination that

the managerial hierarchy proved, under certain conditions, to be more efficient than other institutional arrangements.[6]

This approach highlights the complex interaction between the development of relatively homogeneous mass markets, mass production technology and specialised legal practices, which generated the 'organisational imperatives' most efficiently served by management bureaucracies.[7] While this interaction worked out at a different pace and in different ways – consequently producing differing historical trajectories for the evolution of managerial hierarchies in different industries and/or countries – an underlying efficiency dynamic is seen to be at work:

> Fundamentally, scheduling through managerial hierarchy promised higher and more stable profits than earlier arrangements, mostly by lowering unit costs and stabilizing capacity utilization. . . . Hierarchical scheduling of multiunit systems, in turn, led to the development of organizational structures and control systems to monitor the units. Much of the competitive advantage of hierarchies over markets . . . depends on their ability to provide effective and relatively cheap supervision of performance and use of resources.[8]

The explanation of managerial hierarchies offered above contrasts with a second view linking organisational development in managerial forms directly to the increasing power exercised by managerial élites in societies dominated by corporate institutions and groups – irrespective of the peculiarities of their economic systems. In this way, the strategic significance of corporate management structures within both private and public sector bureaucracies is traced to the political power accruing to managers as a result of the indispensable socio-technical functions they perform:

> The managerial world view sees an industrial society as a network of controlling and subordinate organizations, each dominated by elites who attempt to manage resources and extend their domain of control. New forms of domination have replaced older capitalist structures. Corporate and managerial power has become more important than capital or a capitalist class in structuring the relations between state and economy.[9]

This characterisation of the development of modern management forms in terms of the political dominance of corporate élites (in *all* sectors of society) over subordinate groups – such as private owners, rank and file workers or individual citizens – is predicated on the belief in bureaucratic rationalisation as a universal feature of industrial societies. The rapid extension of functional differentiation and structural complexity within such societies is seen to produce an irresistible tendency towards the organised co-ordination and control of all forms of collective social action. It is these organisational structures that provide managers with their power base from which they come to dominate modern industrial societies:

> In the managerial perspective, power is derived from the organization of authority in which decisions are made, that is, structures. The ability to create effective organizations outside the state transforms social groups into dominant interest groups with the capacity to control or create particular forms of state organization, securing continuous access to the centers of power. Because dominant interests and the state organize around each other to secure reciprocal access, the internal organization of the state and the external organization of dominant interest groups tend to be homogenous.[10]

Thus the dominant role of bureaucratic organisation in modern corporate systems has fundamentally transformed the structure of industrial societies towards institutionalised interest group representation independent of class identity and affiliation.[11] In turn, these bureaucratic organisations are the instruments of control created by a managerial élite determined to establish and maintain its political dominance within a corporate system that is seen to depend for its very survival – much less its continued economic success – upon the socio-technical expertise provided by its creators.[12]

The third explanation for the historical development of management structures consisting of a specialised functional division of labour, co-ordinated through a formal authority hierarchy, directs its attention to the imperatives of class domination and control:

> The expansion of the factory, or the 'capitalist work place', separate from the home, as Pollard and others have shown in the case of Britain, was due more to the perceived needs of

employers to secure regularized labour discipline than to the sheer technical effectiveness of the factory. Surveillance in the capitalistic enterprise is the key to management. . . . The emergence of disciplined labour was thus very closely intertwined with the increasingly successful creation of modes of industrial management, operating with a variety of partly novel techniques of surveillance.[13]

The proposition that the development of managerial organisation is a consequence of the need for capitalist employers to control the work performance of factory labour in a detailed and disciplined fashion is supported by Marglin[14] and Clawson.[15] Marglin contends that the key to the success of factory organisation under managerial surveillance 'was the substitution of capitalists' for workers' control of the production process; discipline and supervision could and did reduce costs *without* being technologically superior'.[16] On the contrary, Marglin continues, technological change was shaped and determined by a form of factory organisation dominated by managerial hierarchies of co-ordination and control. Managerial surveillance and labour discipline were class issues rather than matters of technological efficiency, in that their absence could be disastrous for profit levels without necessarily being inefficient from the point of view of production costs.

Clawson's analysis of the bureaucratisation of the labour process in American industry between 1860 and 1920 also supports this class control explanation of managerial organisation. He firmly rejects the inevitability argument for the development of managerial bureaucracy in the state and in industry, which he equates with the logic of explanation offered by American organisation theorists such as Perrow[17] and Blau.[18] While the latter explain bureaucratic structures as the inevitable administrative correlates of large-scale and technologically complex production systems, Clawson maintains that the historical development of these structures must be explained in terms of the need for detailed and systematic control of the work process under modern capitalism:

The view of bureaucracy as a control mechanism . . . sees its origins in the realization of capital that so long as capital relied on general rules and directives too much control was left in workers' hands. Capitalist factories had long had rules and regulations, a division of labour, and hierarchy, and formally they had always been dictatorships. Bureaucracy was created as a way of moving beyond such general directives to specific detailed control of the work process.[19]

The technical efficiency, political power and class control explanations for the rise of modern management structures are mutually exclusive to the extent that they assign explanatory primacy to very different sets of factors in the historical accounts that they provide. However, this does not preclude our recognising the contributory status of additional factors that are only afforded – at best – secondary significance within formalised explanatory logics. Chandler, for instance, admits that:

> Once a managerial hierarchy had successfully increased profits by co-ordinating operations, it became in itself a source of power, permanence and continued growth. . . . As enterprises grew, and as the number of executives increased, managers became more specialized and professional. . . . Salaried managers' specialized knowledge and their firms' ability to generate the funds necessary for continued expansion meant that they soon controlled the destiny of the enterprises by which they were employed.[20]

This clearly indicates a recognition of the complex interaction between efficiency and power factors in stimulating and sustaining the trend towards complex managerial hierarchies. Gospel's review of the development of labour management strategies in Britain since the industrial revolution echoes the need to unravel the subtle interdependence between economic, political and class factors that produced a 'long-term, though hesitant, trend towards the elaboration of integrated internal hierarchies'.[21] Teulings's structuralist account of the development of differentiated management with separate, and often conflicting, decision-making rationalities, begins with the proposition that:

> management owes its existence to the possibility of transferring the co-ordinating and allocating function of market mechanisms to administrative/managerial structures. The rise of 'the managers' can, in essence, be considered as the rise of a new economic function: the *administrative* co-ordination and allocation of capital and labour.[22]

Consequently, it is not a question of competitive efficiency *or*

political *or* class struggle in providing an explanation of the historical development of modern management as a specific organisational form. As Storey[23] concludes, these factors are interdependent in
the sense that the emergence of management as a distinctive social
practice performed by a specialist group of practitioners must be
accounted for in terms of the dynamic interaction between the technical, economic, political and social factors that produced industrial
or managerial capitalism as a distinctive socio-economic system.

The predominant concern in this book is the control function that
management fulfils within the conflicting interests and values between social groups and classes contending within capitalist work
organisation. However, the dynamic of power struggles between
contending groups and classes in which management is necessarily
implicated clearly has major implications for the way in which
efficiency and political factors interpenetrate to 'select among
different forms of the division of labour and thus shape the particular forms of social production and reproduction'.[24]

This latter issue – that is, the ideological constructions that inform
and underlie different, not to say competing, definitions of 'efficiency' – takes us on to the theme of managerial ideologies.

MANAGERIAL IDEOLOGIES

The growth of modern management as a unique organisational
form was paralleled by the construction and promulgation of frameworks of beliefs and values through which managerial claims to
social status and power could be legitimated. However, the relationship between organisational and ideological development was often
untidy and fragmented. Any assumption of a deterministic relationship between structural transformation and ideological reconstruction was belied by evidence of a process characterised by
semi-autonomous development and the need for adaptability on
both sides.[25]

This section will briefly review the attempts that have been made
to understand the complex interaction between organisational and
ideological change in management. It will provide the background
to a more detailed consideration – in the following section – of
empirical work conducted on managerial behaviour within corporate hierarchies.

Bendix defines ideologies of management as 'ideas concerning work, the authority of employers and the reasons for subordination'.[26] As such:

they are articulated in response to the logic of authority relationships in economic enterprises and formed through a constant process of formulation and reformation by which spokesmen identified with a social group seek to articulate what they sense to be its shared understandings.[27]

In this sense, managerial ideologies are considered as frameworks of ideas 'which are espoused by or for those who exercise authority in economic enterprises and which seek to explain and justify that authority'.[28] This conception of managerial ideologies closely links together institutional and ideological development in that it treats the latter as 'a response to the problems of co-ordination and direction in large-scale enterprises'.[29]

Consequently, the sociological analysis of managerial ideologies must be related to the analysis of managerial organisation. The former provide the legitimations – however partial and contradictory – on and through which organisational arrangements can be institutionalised. As Bendix puts it:

In modern industry management has had to concern itself, ideologically and practically, with industrial organization and labour management as major problems over and above the technical, financial and marketing aspects of the enterprise.[30]

His analysis of changes in management ideologies in Anglo-American societies over a period of two centuries suggests a long-term process of bureaucratisation whereby 'management subjects the conditions of employment to an impersonal systematisation, while the employees seek to modify the implementation of the rules in a manner they regard as advantageous to themselves'.[31] Developments in managerial ideology reflected the increasing bureaucratisation of economic enterprises in that the values of collective teamwork and organisational integration – as represented in the human relations ideology – superseded the Darwinian struggle for survival and the pursuit of self-interest central to Taylorism.[32]

Subsequent analysis[33] also points to the continuing ideological appeal of an organicist philosophy stressing organisational integration and equilibrium deftly maintained by a managerial élite schooled in the arcane theories and techniques of social engineering. Between the late 1930s and mid-1960s this human relations ideology was reworked within a more sophisticated theoretical apparatus, which treated organisations as complex social systems directed and controlled by managerial experts who balanced out the conflicting demands of organisational imperatives and individual needs.[34] As Anthony puts it, by the 1960s the central principle of managerial ideology had become:

> integration and the subordination of the individual's goals to those of the organization that employs him. . . . The human engineering which is advocated by the new science of management is aimed at achieving large-scale changes in society in order to facilitate business objectives. . . . The end result is achieved when the application of authority and power is no longer necessary to assist in the achievement of the organization's goals because the goals have been internalized by those who are to pursue them.[35]

This view reflects Child's conclusion that management thought has served two major ideological functions. First, to serve and defend the dominance of management 'by asserting that managerial objectives and behaviour were in accordance with widely accepted social values'.[36] Second, to extend managerial control through widespread acceptance of the belief that managers have the moral duty and technical expertise necessary to design and implement major institutional changes in the existing social order.[37]

However, the recent study by Nichols[38] of the implementation of a 'work humanisation' programme at one of the chemical processing plants of a large multi-national corporation neatly illustrates the practical limits of neo-human relations ideology when it comes face-to-face with the political realities of capitalist workplace organisation. The latter – in the shape of shop-floor conflict, intra-managerial power struggles, coercive systems of social control and the demand for profitable production – provided the structural parameters within which work humanisation programmes have to operate. Job-enrichment schemes, worker-participation experiments and semi-autonomous work groups on the shop-floor had to be adapted to the structures and systems through which management attempted to control a recalcitrant labour force that did not automatically accept its subordination within the labour process.

This study also raises the general issue of the problematic relationship between managerial ideology and practice as it relates to the empirical research conducted on managerial work within corporate structures. It is this theme that provides the focus for the following section.

THE NATURE OF MANAGERIAL WORK[39]

The image of managerial work as an objective scientific activity concerned with achieving a rational alignment between organisational ends and means has exerted a powerful influence on the development of management thought. This is so to the extent that such an idealised representation continued to send out a powerful ideological afterglow – tinged with the aura of a neutral technocracy or profession exercising authority on behalf of the general good – long after its mythical character had been cruelly exposed by empirical research. Thus, the Platonic ideal of managerial work, conveyed in classical management theory, continued to find expression – if in very different theoretical idioms and conceptual vocabularies – in the ostensibly more sophisticated analytical frameworks developed in the 1950s and 1960s.[40] The manager was transformed from a philosopher king into a faceless technocrat who exchanged moral collectivism for scientific rationality.

The conception of management as a neutral technocracy or profession controlling complex organisations in the interests of society as a whole was considerably broadened to include a far wider range of 'socio-technical' variables to that traditionally found within the ambit of the classical approach. The skilful diagnosis and therapeutic treatment of socio-psychological problems became as important as the technical expertise required in formal organisational design. Yet, modern-day systems or contingency theory still conveyed the image of managerial work as a social practice characterised by rational planning and control unencumbered by ideological prejudice or material vested interest.[41]

However, between the early 1950s and 1970s a number of empirical studies were carried out that severely dented this ideal image. By the late 1970s, alternative conceptions of managerial work that completely broke with the rational scientific paradigm had come on to the sociological agenda and were beginning to exert a widening influence beyond the limiting institutional confines of higher education.[42]

The first wave of empirical research, which lapped against the theoretical hull of the rational scientific paradigm and slowly but surely began to rust its conceptual rivets, focused upon patterned diversity and variation revealed in both the form and context of managerial jobs.[43] Hales suggests that we can detect a number of underlying themes in this body of empirical work – beginning with Carlson's pioneering study of ten Swedish executives in 1951[44] and culminating in Mintzberg's observational study of five American chief executives in 1973.[45]

First, these studies revealed the highly contingent and diverse characteristic of managerial work – that is, variations in the different configurations of elements, processes, contact patterns and time allocations constituting managerial jobs were contingent upon functional, hierarchical, organisational and environmental location. Second, they indicated that managerial jobs were 'sufficiently loosely defined to be highly negotiable and susceptible to choice of both style and content'.[46] Choices relating both to job content and to job form were evident, argues Hales, as a recurring motif reflected in other activities – but within the constraints presented by organisational and environmental location.[47] Third, the studies suggested that the activities that constituted managerial practice were characterised by a high degree of pressure and conflict, so that the ability and capacity to negotiate acceptable performances in the face of competing, even contradictory, demands were necessary prerequisites for the successful managerial negotiation of social order.[48] Fourth, they convey the clear impression that, by its very nature, a great deal of managerial work is an automatic response to prevailing circumstances. As Hales puts it: 'The manager is less a slow and methodical decision-maker, more a "doer" who has to react rapidly to problems as they arise, "thinks on his feet", takes decisions *in situ* and develops a preference for concrete activities'.[49] Finally, these studies show that the gap between management practice and theory – at least as represented in the rational scientific paradigm – is very considerable indeed.[50] Far from constituting an exercise in long-term rational planning and control, the reality of managerial work approximates much more closely to the model of 'disjointed incrementalism' adumbrated by Lindblom.[51] As Stewart concludes:

The common description of a manager as one who plans, organizes, co-ordinates, motivates, and controls suggests a logical, ordered process where these different activities can be distinguished by the individual, or by an observer, and where the manager has time to devote to planning. The picture that emerges from studies of what managers do is of someone who lives in a whirl of activity, in which attention must be switched every few minutes from one subject, problem and person to another; of an uncertain world where relevant information includes gossip and speculation about how other people are thinking and what they are likely to do; and where it is necessary, particularly in the more senior posts, to develop a network of people who can fill one in on what is going on and what is likely to happen.[52]

The second wave of empirical research (often running contermi-nous with the first wave) highlighted the political character of managerial activity, in that it revealed the crucial significance of power processes and relations for the routine accomplishment of managerial work.[53] Studies such as those conducted by Gouldner,[54] Dalton,[55] Burns and Stalker,[56] Sayles,[57] Pettigrew[58] and Kotter[59] documented the alliances that managers have to form with other individuals and interest groups, within and without their employing organisation, in order to negotiate a viable route between the conflicting pressures and corresponding uncertainties that are the very stuff of organisational life. This negotiation demands high-level skills in constructing and reconstructing organisational net-works and agendas through which interpersonal dependencies can be established and the legitimacy of personal aims secured. Expert-ise in the use of informational and symbolic resources, as well as in the manipulation of formal organisational designs, becomes the *sine qua non* of managerial success.

More recently, a third wave of research has begun to appear, which concentrates on the symbolic aspects of managerial work and their vital contribution to the realisation of moral and political legitimacy within work organisations.[60] This research presents a view of management as a social collectivity through which a subcul-ture of shared meanings is constructed, preserved and transmitted from one generation to another. These shared meanings are de-ployed to generate and maintain common 'moral and political environments' in which necessary political deals and compromises can be balanced against the moral dilemmas that confront individual managers in the everyday performance of their roles. As Gowler and Legge suggest:

> the fact that managers spend a great deal of their time talking is more than a matter for passing comment, and not necessarily something to be deplored. This endless talk, especially the rhetoric, may be the way in which social control is maintained while, in situations of great uncertainty and complexity, managerial prerogatives are simultaneously accomplished and legitimated. This is not an inconsiderable achievement. Indeed, this may be what 'achievement' is really all about.[61]

As this quotation suggests, most of the research conducted on the management of symbolic meanings focuses upon the structures of domination and control that are perpetuated through the elaboration and communication of collective myths that stabilise and support existing institutional orders. Thus, managers are seen to be routinely engaged in propagating notions such as 'managerial prerogative', 'managerial effectiveness' and 'managerial accountability', the object being to create, sustain, and justify a structure of power relations in which their authority is secured. As Pettigrew indicates: 'The management of meaning refers to a process of symbol construction and value use designed both to create legitimacy for one's actions, ideas and demands, and to delegitimise the demands of one's opponents'.[62]

However, research on the management of meaning has also highlighted the extremely precarious and ambiguous nature of the collective myths through which organisational order is constructed and maintained. This is so to the extent that it has brought out the internal tensions and contradictions embodied in symbolic orders and in the processes through which they constructed.[63] It has also displayed the 'strategies of myth management' that managers are required to deploy in the event of fundamental changes in existing power structures that call into question the legitimacy previously provided by established or 'official' myths and values.[64] In situations such as these – that is, characterised by deep-seated change and the uncertainties that it generates – managers will not have the option of incrementally reconstructing dominant systems of meaning. They will be forced into a more 'revolutionary' transformation of conventional ideologies and myths. This is likely to entail great risks to the prevailing structure of power relations and its legitimatory rationale within the work organisation.[65]

The empirical research that we have been reviewing in this section involves a dramatic shift away from the rational scientific paradigm of managerial work and the conceptions that it embodies. Not only is the general character of managerial work seen to be fundamentally different from that enshrined in the latter, but also the whole conceptual basis of the technocratic view is seriously undermined. Managerial work undergoes a conceptual meta-morphosis and emerges on the other side as a social practice that is unavoidably implicated – in a very deep and enduring way – in the messy, not to say dirty, business whereby existing structures of power and control are maintained in the face of conflicts and tensions that – potentially at least – threaten their material and cultural foundations. Having exchanged the role of philosopher king for that of a neutral technocrat engaged in the rational design, implementation and evaluation of organisational systems, the manager once more changes into a Machiavellian-type charac-ter immersed in the micro-politics of institutional order and control.[66]

As one might expect, this body of research – and the general conclusions drawn from it about the nature of managerial work – has not been immune to criticism. The major sociological criticism concerns the lack of an institutional dimension to much of this research, in the sense that it has neglected 'the institutional grounds of managerial work as an expression of politico-economic relations of power'.[67] Consequently, more recent research is still seen to encourage a 'de-contextualised' view of managerial work in that it perpetuates a continuing reluctance to relate managerial practice to 'the wider context of labour processes and the social division of labour'.[68]

We shall look at this issue in greater detail in Chapter five.[69] The review that has been provided of recent research on managerial work does, however, establish a broader intellectual context in which a more focused discussion of different levels of management within the corporate hierarchy can be developed in the following section.

THE MANAGERIAL ELITE[70]

The inner sanctum of the company boardroom and the senior management enclaves within corporate hierarchies still remain a largely closed and secretive world to sociologists. With some notable exceptions, sociological research on management work has tended to focus on the trials and tribulations of middle- and lower-level management. The more rarified atmosphere of strategic management has proved to be extremely thin and relatively inhospitable to the revealing, and potentially disturbing, investigations of sociologists interested in the behaviour of the business/managerial élite.

However, this situation is beginning to change as sociologists direct their attention more closely on the characteristic patterns of work behaviour and relations discovered among directors and senior managers. In this section we will review this work and consider its implications for our understanding of the business/managerial élite within the broader context set by the overview of empirical studies on managerial work carried out in the previous section.

In many respects, the research that has been conducted on the work behaviour and relations of directors and senior managers reflects the patterns that emerged from more general research. The gap between theory and practice revealed by the latter is mirrored in the empirical studies that have been conducted on the business/managerial élite. Mace contrasts the classical functions of boards of directors – strategy formulation, corporate planning and organisational monitoring – with what they actually do in practice:

> In most companies boards of directors serve as a source of advice and counsel, serve as some sort of discipline, and act in crisis situations if the president dies suddenly or is asked to resign because of unsatisfactory management performance . . . boards of directors of most large and medium-sized companies do not establish objectives, strategies and policies, however defined.[71]

Mangham's study suggests that the social reality of executive behaviour departs sharply from the 'tightly scripted, thoroughly rehearsed, minutely directed naturalistic piece of theatre'[72] assumed in most formalistic conceptions of élite conduct in business organisations. Indeed, executive action at this level is seen as a performing art directed at the reconciliation of conflicting interests and values that depends for its success upon a combination of political, theatrical and technical skills geared to the simultaneous maintenance of stability and the generation of innovative capacity. It is practised within an organisational setting defined by ambiguity and uncertainty of the shifting criteria through which performance will be assessed and rewarded. This setting also constitutes a political arena in which power struggles and relations will be crucial factors in shaping executive behaviour.

Such a view of élite conduct is also conveyed in the analysis by Burns and Stalker[73] of the role of the director/senior manager in a number of business organisations that underwent rapid socio-technical change in the 1950s. In this context, the role of the managing director in interpreting technical and commercial developments, as well as adapting the work organisation and employee commitments to a changed situation, became absolutely vital for business success. Yet, in most of the companies that Burns and Stalker studied, senior executives failed to provide the 'institutional statesmanship' required to effect the move from rigid mechanistic structures to more open and fluid organic structures. They tended to cling to 'the old form of the managerial system because it provided protection against the involvements the new order demanded of them'.[74] In part, this was due to the socially – and often physically – isolated positions senior executives occupied at the apex of the managerial hierarchy. However, it also related to their inability to cope effectively with a novel organisational setting in which personal anxiety and insecurity, interest group conflict, and power struggles inside and outside the managerial élite were everyday factors.

Research by Winkler[75] and Pettigrew[76] supports this interpretation of the realities of élite behaviour in corporate hierarchies. Winkler describes a pattern of directors' work defined in terms of physical and social isolation interspersed by periodic military-style inspections of outlying plants or offices. Social segregation inside and outside work was the prevailing pattern so that workers and their problems were consigned to a residual category to be dealt with by industrial relations specialists. Thus workers – and shareholders – were treated by directors almost exclusively as a cost to be minimised as far as possible in the interest of company efficiency and profitability.[77] The sources of information from which directors gleaned knowledge about industrial relations problems depended largely on personal networks, previous experience and mass media stereotypes rather than more systematic communication and information channels within the normal management hierarchy. Winkler concluded that this preference for social isolation, disinterest in industrial relations matters and ignorance of workers' problems was, in part at least, an intentional strategy followed by directors to cope with uncontrollable situations and obstreperous people through a mixture of withdrawal, avoidance and delegation.

Pettigrew's study of strategic change in ICI depicts main boardroom-level behaviour characterised by conservatism, intense political rivalry and fragmented thinking focused on short-term problem-solving rather than integrated strategic thinking. The impetus for change came from lower levels of the management hierarchy and specialist groups directed by the charismatic leadership provided by particular individuals such as John Harvey-Jones, who eventually became chairman in November 1981 after a protracted period of corporate infighting. He had realised very early on that the main board of ICI could not provide the financial, market and technical integration that the company so desperately needed. His approach had been to develop and implement a long-term strategy of 'improving the flow of disconfirming information to the main board about its and the ICI's group's role and processes',[78] while simultaneously building political alliances favourably disposed to change below the level of the main board.

Pfeffer's[79] review of the research on the organisational politics of executive succession and its consequences for lower-level managers reveals a process in which the interplay between power struggles and cultural/ideological debates about the organisation's future is the dominant factor. Both the choice of new chief executives and the subsequent actions that are taken to solidify and institutionalise their power bases illustrate the continuing relevance of political and symbolic processes for an understanding of élite behaviour in business organisations.

However, we must not exaggerate this one-sided interpretation of executive behaviour to the extent that directors and senior managers appear as the weak and conservative playthings of subordinate managers expert in the darker arts of organisational politics.

Indeed, research by Pahl and Winkler,[80] Fidler[81] and Scott[82] provides a very useful corrective to an interpretation of the managerial élite, one that drastically underestimates its capacity to structure the wider organisational setting in which middle and first-line managers operate.

Pahl and Winkler's study of company directors distinguished between proforma boards and functioning boards. The former existed simply to conform with the demands of company law and possessed no consultative or decision-making capacity. The latter played operational roles in companies of varying degrees of magnitude and scope.[83] In companies with functioning boards a subtle form of manipulative collusion between directors, senior managers and middle-level experts took place in order to shape the strategic financial parameters (investment decisions, profit levels, asset growth rates) within which operational decisions about routine resource allocations were made.[84] Manipulation and control of information was the key process for understanding this collusive relationship:

> Successful manipulation in this way depends on the skilful structuring of the information which the board has available for assessing proposals. The power which the managers exercise over boards is power based on information control. Essential to such power is the sealing off of any sources of contradictory information. . . . The answers to the questions 'Who initiated?', 'Who is ultimately responsible for a given decision?', 'Who has power?', 'Who controls?' will be buried by the normal priorities of organizational politics. . . . Once we recognize the processes of manipulation, screening and pre-emption, then any serious consideration of decision-making must allow that decisions may be thrust up from below.[85]

The central role of directors in assessing and balancing the competing interests involved in making major decisions about resource allocation is also reflected in Fidler's research on the social imagery of the British business élite. While denying that the latter is homogeneous in socio-economic and ideological terms,[86] Fidler identifies an overall trend in social imagery as portrayed through the 'balancing interests' ethos:

The main board director is portrayed as balancing the interests of shareholder, the employee, the customer and even
the nation; but these interests are seen to clash only in the
short-term; in the long-term, they coincide and the long-term
pursuit of profit is seen as being to the benefit of all parties.[87]

Scott has provided a general characterisation of the role of the
'dominant coalition' of directors and senior managers in large-scale
business corporations in terms of the effective pursuit of long-term
profitability, constrained by external market forces and by the
internal struggle for power between conflicting interest groups. In
this way, the corporate strategies formulated by the managerial
élite are the outcomes:

> of the alliances and conflicts among the capitalists who make
> up the 'dominant coalition' of each enterprise; but the actions
> of this coalition are shaped by the network of intercorporate
> relations in which the enterprise is embedded and, beyond
> this, by the actions of the state and other political agencies and
> by both organized and unorganized workers. Different groups
> within the dominant coalition may seek to realize conflicting
> corporate strategies, reflecting their conflicting interests as
> well as by conflicts with outside interests which seek to
> influence it. Corporate strategy, therefore, is the result of a
> continual, though sometimes latent, struggle for control.[88]

This analysis is in keeping with the call by Whitley[89] for a
sociology of business firm behaviour that focuses on the decision-
making rationales followed by teams of directors and senior managers in large-scale business corporations within the wider competitive processes and structures in which the latter operate. Such a
focus, he suggests, will help to reveal the underlying managerial
rationalities[90] of particular dominant coalitions in specific firms
and/or industries. These rationalities will inform decision-making
processes and outcomes relating to the acquisition, divestment and
transformation of the productive resources on which the corporation depends. Their analysis needs:

> to incorporate an understanding of how management teams
> co-ordinate and direct resource allocation, rather than simply
> presume they do so by virtue of their position. The social
> processes by which management teams secure adherence and

maintain control of human and material resources have to be specified, if we are to understand fully how and why firms act as they do.[91]

The picture of the work behaviour and relations of the managerial élite that emerges from this review of empirical studies is one of a highly complex – and often divided – group attempting to secure long-term profitability in the face of environmental uncertainty and organisational conflict. While they exercise effective control over strategic resource allocation, usage and direction in business corporations, their power is enmeshed within political structures and processes outside and inside the particular organisational units they dominate. As such, they are intimately locked into the competition and conflicts between managerial sub-cultures and organisational groupings taking place within business firms on a routine basis. A public image of standing above the hue and cry of intercorporate and intracorporate power politics is belied by a private reality in which conflict and struggle over control of the strategic parameters in which firms will operate is an everyday reality.[92]

This assessment clearly raises the question of the relationship between strategic managers located at the apex of the corporate hierarchy on the one hand and operational managers situated at lower levels of the organisation's authority structure on the other. This question can be broached only after some discussion of the research that has been conducted on the work behaviour and relations found amongst middle and first-line managers.

MIDDLE MANAGERS

The rapid expansion of managerial positions and groupings located below the level of the managerial élite and above that of front-line supervisors is closely associated with the internal bureaucratisation of economic enterprises. The latter process involved 'the increasing subdivision of the functions which the owner-managers of the early enterprises had performed personally in the course of their daily routine'.[93] Thus, the bureaucratisation of industrial organisations entailed 'a detailed subdivision of administrative organisation in the enterprise, and such subdivision involves by definition a considerable increase in the number of jobs between the top and bottom of the administrative hierarchy'.[94]

The extension of internal bureaucratic hierarchies within economic enterprises during the late nineteenth and early twentieth centuries 'meant the insertion of a stratum of white-collar workers and technicians between the employer and the shop-floor, diminishing the role and status of the old sub-contractor and the traditional foremen'.[95] This stratum of middle-level positions and groupings performed an ever-widening range of functions concerned both with direct control over productive activity and indirect support tasks focused on company welfare programmes and technical innovation.[96]

In this sense, middle management is a product of organisational differentiation to the extent that it developed out of the increasing complexity of the internal division of labour with economic enterprises and the control problems this created for employers. At the same time, the wide range of functions and tasks performed by middle managers are broadly concerned with achieving overall co-ordination and integration of the specialised units that constitute the modern business corporation.[97] They administer the organisational bureaucracy, and its associated social control technology, which created them. They also ensure that the corporation is equipped to deal with the economic, technical, social and political demands made by a harsh and unforgiving business environment. Located within that broad organisational expanse of levels and positions between first-line supervision and top executives, middle management provides the operational control, technical expertise and specialist support so vital to the continued functioning of the modern business corporation.[98]

Much of the empirical research carried out on the work behaviour and relations of middle managers suggests that the initiation and regulation of inter-group conflict through political bargaining and negotiation is the central component of their role.[99] The reconciliation of conflicting demands through the skilful deployment of material, technical and symbolic resources to achieve overall co-ordination of interdependent activities necessary for continued operation provides the *raison d'être* of their organisational existence.

Fox provides an illuminating summary of the work situation of middle managers and the tensions it entails:

The position of middle managers is a complex one. They are

likely to feel their location in the social organization to be more congruent for their aspirations than do those at the bottom of the hierarchy. Yet their goals are certainly not identical with those of top management. Their dependence upon higher management for approval, support and promotion is itself a differentiating factor, for dependence introduces its own frame of reference which by definition cannot be shared by those upon whom the dependence rests. Another factor distinguishing middle management from its superiors is its more immediate exposure to the day-to-day pressures on the shop floor. These two factors alone may result in goals which relate less to top management goals than to a satisfactory personal accommodation of conflicting pressures from above and below.[100]

Both Kay[101] and Shorris[102] support this interpretation to the extent that their research conveys a picture of growing insecurity, powerlessness, inflexibility and isolation in the face of intensifying pressure from below and continuing disinterest – not to say hostility – from above. In this situation, the need for the middle manager to build and maintain alliances between coalitions of interest groups both within and outside the employing organisation is a necessary prerequisite for organisational survival, as well as for the effective performance of their regulative or integrative function.

Indeed, some commentators have provided an extremely depressing view of the longer-term prospects for middle management – or at least that part of middle management that forms the organisational backbone of the line hierarchy and is excluded from membership of either the technostructure or support staff through its lack of formal qualifications and accredited technical expertise.[103] Declining career prospects, the deskilling effect of new technology, systematic exclusion from organisational positions requiring formally recognised credentials and the longer-term impact of rationalisation processes replacing 'tacit knowledge' with standardised techniques produce a situation in which the middle ranks of the line hierarchy are substantially thinned out.[104] As such, it is predicted that they will suffer the fate previously experienced by foremen. The intricate and delicate web of political relationships and understandings that middle managers constructed and maintained in order to facilitate operational continuity will be swept away by a more sophisticated and precise control technology administered by professional experts. The organisational need they fulfilled and the ideological legitimation its performance provided will both be made obsolete by the widespread introduction of standardised control systems designed and operated by a rising cadre of professional experts more closely aligned with the material interests and ideological frameworks of top management.[105] The highly personalised or indeterminate social and political skills utilised by middle-line managers in their task of integrating subordinates effectively within the productive process are transformed into standardised control packages through which operational coordination can be more easily routinised. Consequently, middle-line managers are subjected to the same process of bureaucratic rationalisation and technical control once reserved for their subordinates.

Recent research has concentrated on inter-professional conflict within middle management and its impact on the evolution of managerial control strategies.[106] The development of specialist functions within the technical component of middle management – such as accountancy, personnel management, marketing, operational research and design engineering – is interpreted as a general process whereby professional groups achieve upward mobility within the corporate hierarchy by providing techniques that offer effective responses to the periodic economic crises top-level management face in their role as agents of capitalist accumulation. Some groups are more successful than others in engaging on collective mobility projects to the extent that they are able to achieve monopoly control over a highly specialised knowledge base and professional practice that seems to meet the requirements of the economic crises faced by senior management.

Thus, accountants have been much more successful than engineers in establishing and protecting their dominant political position within the management hierarchies of British and American[107] companies. They have been able to monopolise control of a professional practice shrouded in technical mystique and indeterminacy,[108] and to convince top management of the strategic relevance of their highly specialised knowledge and skills for the operation of profitable production. Engineers, on the other hand, have been unable to develop their knowledge base and professional practice into a comprehensive control strategy they can monopolise and manipulate to achieve upward organisational mobility. Traditionally accorded a low status within Anglo-American management, internally divided and producing a knowledge base and professional practice that can be poached by other specialisms, engineers remain in a subordinate position more closely related to their colleagues in the middle ranks of the line hierarchy.

However, even those specialist groups that have achieved upward mobility within corporate hierarchies are experiencing a process of internal differentiation and fragmentation along hierarchical and functional lines. The more successful a specialist group is in realising upward corporate mobility as a result of effective monopolisation and legitimation of its knowledge base and skills, the more likely it is to become internally stratified into an élite that retains control over 'the esoteric indeterminate aspects of professional practice, while delegating the routine aspects to subordinates'.[109] This simply seems to reproduce the strong tendency towards internal differentiation and segmentation that has always existed within middle management from its inception as a check upon the relatively unfettered powers of foremen in early-twentieth-century-manufacturing industry.

It is to the position of first-line managers and their declining position in contemporary managerial hierarchies that we must now turn in completing our review of managerial work.

FIRST-LINE MANAGERS

By the early decades of the twentieth century the directly employed foreman had become the dominant figure in workshop management.[110] The power and authority of the traditional foreman to control and direct subordinate labour in pursuit of maximum production had emerged out of the decay of internal subcontracting.[111] As Littler puts it:

> the traditional foreman was the undisputed master of his own shop, and like the internal contractor before him, he hired and fired, set wages, planned and allocated work. However, there were fundamental differences between the contractor and the traditional foreman: the foreman did not employ his own labour, his wage or salary was his main source of income, and

he did not have the same petty capitalist interest in costs and profits.[112]

The foundations of the foreman's authority rested on a combination of technical proficiency, administrative expertise, social skill and physical power. His pre-eminence in the process of labour management seemed secure as long as he remained the primary source of the work rules through which workshop order was secured and the judicial authority by which work discipline was maintained.

However, the 'foreman's power started to be modified almost as soon as it had emerged from the decay of internal contract'.[113] While his considerable power to control and direct subordinate labour continued into the inter-war period, the pressure on senior management to rationalise production systems and bureaucratise employment relations led to a situation in which there was a 'gradual trend to shift various functions which had traditionally been the foreman's to centralised staff departments'.[114] Senior management needed to break – or more realistically 'fracture' – the foreman's power to ensure more effective control over the production process and the manner in which labour was utilised.[115] The major organisational mechanism developed to achieve this objective was a stratum of middle managers and technicians that made significant inroads into the supervisory role.[116] Increasingly, the foreman became subject to the same centralised control systems previously reserved for shop-floor workers.

Indeed, by the 1940s the decline of the workshop foreman and his metamorphosis into a plethora of supervisory positions subject to the dictates of centralised functional departments had reached a crisis point.

The supervisor was now seen to be the 'man in the middle' caught between the opposing forces of management and shopfloor, torn by competing demands and loyalties. The supervisor's role had become more stressful and his capacity to achieve what management expected of him progressively more limited. The continued development of centralized functional departments, laying down a framework of procedures which governed many shop-floor parameters, and the encouragement they gave for shop-stewards to bypass the supervisor, led other commentators to conclude that he no longer occupied a position of special importance in the management system. He was more a transmitter of management decisions than an active participant in them.[117]

Between the 1940s and 1960s a number of studies attempted to assess the position of the first-line manager in contemporary work organisations.[118] Two – often competing – interpretations of the present position of and future prospects for first-line managers emerged from this research. First, the 'man in the middle' thesis, which suggested that the first-line manager was caught in a position of severe role conflict. Incompatible pressures from senior management and workers had combined with irreversible structural changes in work organisations to produce a situation in which 'the foreman has become powerless to control or to influence his situation'.[119] Second, the 'marginal man' thesis, which indicated that the role of the first-line manager had shrunk to a point where it had become largely irrelevant to the actual functioning of work organisations.[120]

Empirical support has been found for both of these interpretations. Child and Partridge give general backing to the 'man in the middle' thesis to the extent that the supervisors they studied 'were in the middle of things rather than outside the main vertical hierarchy and the main lines of communication'.[121] They had lost much of their managerial authority but remained accountable for satisfactory worker performance in a stressful and demanding work environment where higher management was largely unsympathetic to the problems they faced. The marginalisation thesis receives support from Hill,[122] Nichols and Beynon,[123] and Armstrong.[124] Each of these studies highlights a situation in which the foreman/ supervisory role is subject to rationalising processes that make its traditional labour control function increasingly irrelevant to modern production systems. As a result, the foreman/supervisor's role becomes socially and organisationally marginalised as more complex systems of technical and bureaucratic control expropriate his traditional functions within the labour process.

However, more recent research has challenged both of these interpretations.[125] Rose, *et al.* argue that supervisors still retain considerable power and authority within the workplace:

> they are still widely involved in the allocation of tasks and exert considerable control over the pace and intensity of work. . . . Our evidence suggests that first-line supervisors are

neither entirely marginal to employer-employee relations, nor wholly powerless in their ability to shape the market situations and work situations of subordinates. Not only are supervisors not disappearing: it is also the case that they still wield real power in the workplace . . . independent, direct and authoritative supervision is still a significant element in the apparatus of social control at the point of production. . . . First-line supervisors under advanced capitalism are neither rendered progressively less powerful nor less authoritative.[126]

Harris's[127] perceptive and sensitive 're-study' of the chemical complex that provided the empirical site for the research by Nichols and Beynon also reveals a much more complex picture. Supervisors in the two ammonia plants that she studied enjoyed greater control over the socio-technical system than the proponents of either the middle or marginal theses would suggest. Their social prestige and organisational status was maintained by their continued centrality to effective technical operations and to the efficient utilisation of labour within the production process. Each of these tasks required technical, social and political skills of the highest order, combined with an intense plant loyalty and work commitment that set them apart from senior managers. Neither the obsolete agents of capitalist control nor the powerless and alienated creatures of conflicting social forces, first-line supervisors retained a significant role in the practice of management and the symbolic processes through which it was legitimated.

In this respect, more recent research on first-line managers has provided a useful corrective to analysts who 'tend to attribute to management a greater facility for controlling a workforce by technological or bureaucratic means than it in fact possesses'.[128] While a long-term decline in the power and authority of first-line managers, as well as their increasing isolation from higher levels of management, can be discerned in all of these studies, the speed, uniformity and scale of this process should not be overestimated. Supervisors remain a significant component of the management structure through which the organisation and control of the labour process is routinely achieved. Sociological research and analysis suggests that they should not be consigned to the dustbin of history just yet.

CONCLUSION

This chapter has set an appreciation of sociological research on managerial work within a broader historical and ideological context. In general terms, it has indicated that rationalistic models of managerial work need to be rejected in favour of models that adequately reflect the complexities of the social and organisational worlds that real managers actually inhabit. At the same time, it has warned against analyses that dissolve the structural constraints embedded in managerial practice into a formless process of interpersonal negotiation and compromise.

The reality of management structure emerging from sociological research and analysis is one of a highly stratified social order permeated by relational networks that simultaneously sustain and undermine the viability of the former. While each level of the management hierarchy discussed in the chapter is located within a structure that creates and maintains distinctive sub-cultures, the technical, social and political realities of management practice inevitably subvert the divisions that the former generates. The formal structure may demand a rigid division of labour and cultural separation between different levels of management, but the complexities of management practice require modes of social interaction that severely weaken these barriers. As a result, managerial work must accommodate the conflict between the imperatives of structural differentiation and the requirements of socio-political practice.

This chapter has revealed the ubiquity of social conflict for the individual manager and the practice he or she performs. The theme of managing social conflict is dealt with next.

REFERENCES

1. The reference here is to Pollard, S., *The Genesis of Modern Management* (Arnold, London, 1965).
2. Elaboration of this interpretation is to be found in Chandler, A.D., *The Visible Hand: The Managerial Revolution in American Business* (Harvard University Press, Cambridge, Mass., 1977); Chandler, A.D. and Daems, H. (eds.), *Managerial Hierarchies: Comparative Perspectives on the Rise of the Modern Industrial Enterprise* (Harvard University Press, Cambridge, Mass., 1980); Francis, A., Turk, J. and

Willman, P. (eds.), *Power, Efficiency and Institutions* (Heinemann, London, 1983).
3. Mills, C.W., *The Power Elite* (Oxford University Press, New York, 1956); Burnham, J., *The Managerial Revolution* (Penguin, Harmondsworth, 1942); Galbraith, J.K., *The New Industrial State* (Penguin, Harmondsworth, 1967); Useem, M., *The Inner Circle: Large Corporations and the Rise of Business Political Activity in the U.S. and U.K.* (Oxford University Press, New York, 1984). For an overview of this literature see Alford, R.R. and Friedland, R., *Powers of Theory: Capitalism, the State and Democracy* (Cambridge University Press, New York, 1985).
4. Marglin, S., 'The Origins and Functions of Hierarchy in Capitalist Production', in Nichols, T. (ed.), *Capital and Labour* (Fontana, Glasgow, 1980), pp. 237–54; Clawson, D., *Bureaucracy and the Labour Process* (Monthly Review Press, New York, 1980); Giddens, A., *Social Theory and Modern Sociology* (Polity Press, Oxford, 1987).
5. The threefold analytical distinction suggested here to explain macro-level developments in managerial organisation corresponds to the distinction between technical, political and critical perspectives outlined in Chapter one.
6. Daems, H., 'The Rise of the Modern Industrial Enterprise', in Chandler and Daems, op. cit., (1980), p. 207.
7. This point is developed in greater detail in Chandler, A.D., 'The Development of Modern Management Structure in the U.S. and U.K.', in Hannah, L. (ed.), *Management Strategy and Business Development* (Macmillan, London, 1970), pp. 23–51.
8. Daems, op. cit., (1980), p. 218. For a trenchant critique of this view see Perrow, C., 'Markets, Hierarchies and Hegemony', in Van de Ven, A.H. and Joyce, W.F. (eds.), *Perspectives on Organizational Design and Behaviour* (Wiley, New York, 1981), pp. 371–86.
9. Alford and Friedland, op. cit., (1985), p. 164.
10. Ibid., p. 169.
11. For a development of this point see Schmitter, P., 'Still the Century of Corporatism?', *Review of Politics*, vol. 36, (1974), pp. 85–131.
12. This point is elaborated in greater detail in Burns, T., 'On the Rationale of the Corporate System', in Marris, R. (ed.), *The Corporate Society* (Macmillan, London, 1974), pp. 121–77.
13. Giddens, A., op. cit., (1987), pp. 175–6.
14. Marglin, S., op. cit., (1980).
15. Clawson, D., op. cit., (1980).
16. Marglin, S., op. cit., (1980), p. 239.
17. Perrow, C., *Complex Organizations: A Critical Essay* (Scott Foresman, Illinois, 1972).
18. Blau, P., *On the Nature of Organizations* (Wiley, New York, 1974).
19. Clawson, D., op. cit., (1980), p. 248.
20. Chandler, A.D., 'The United States: Seedbed of Managerial Capitalism', in Chandler, A.D. and Daems, H. (eds.), op. cit., (1980), pp. 9–40 (p. 12).

21. Gospel, H., 'Introduction', in Gospel, H. and Littler, C.R. (eds.), *Managerial Strategies and Industrial Relations* (Heinemann, London, 1983), p. 20. This issue is discussed in greater depth in the next chapter.
22. Teulings, A., 'Managerial Labour Processes in Organized Capitalism: The Power of Corporate Management and the Powerlessness of the Manager', in Knights, D. and Willmott, H. (eds.), *Managing the Labour Process* (Gower, Aldershot, 1986), pp. 142–65.
23. Storey, J., *Managerial Prerogative and the Question of Control* (Routledge and Kegan Paul, London, 1983).
24. Rueschemeyer, D., *Power and the Division of Labour* (Polity Press, Oxford, 1986), p. 171.
25. As Child puts it: 'the case of British management thought illustrates how existing concepts and ideas may exercise an independent role in the formation of systems of thought. This is not to deny that such ideas may subsequently be adapted to suit the requirements of those formulating thought. It is, however, to assert that ideas can, through their own appeal, autonomously influence the content of that thought'. Child, J., *British Management Thought* (Allen and Unwin, London, 1969), p. 235.
26. Bendix, R., *Work and Authority in Industry* (University of California Press, California, 1974), p. xx.
27. Ibid., p. xii.
28. Ibid., p. 2.
29. Ibid., p. 9.
30. Ibid., p. 10. As we shall see, this ideological work has become a central theme in more recent studies of managerial behaviour and organisation.
31. Ibid., p. 247. The second half of this process is dealt with in more detail in Chapter four.
32. Ibid., pp. 338–40. However, Bendix draws a clear distinction between the relative ideological success of human relations ideology and the continuing *practical* import of Taylorite methods of work organisation and control. On this point see Bendix, (1974), pp. 319–31.
33. Baritz, L., *The Servants of Power* (Wiley, New York, 1965); Child, J., op. cit., (1969); Nichols, T., *Ownership, Control and Ideology* (Allen and Unwin, London, 1969); Anthony, P.D., *The Ideology of Work* (Tavistock, London, 1977); Bartell, T., 'The Human Relations Ideology', *Human Relations*, vol. 29, (1976), pp. 731–50; Fox, A., *Man Mismanagement* (Hutchinson, London, 2nd edition, 1985).
34. This development is outlined in greater detail in Reed, M., *Redirections in Organizational Analysis* (Tavistock, London, 1985).
35. Anthony, P.D., op. cit., (1977), p. 228.
36. Child, J., op. cit., (1969), p. 228.
37. Child relates the 'defensive posture' to early-twentieth-century management thought, while the more aggressive, or 'utopian', social engineering strain is equated with more recent developments associated with the rise of applied managerial social science.

38. Nichols, T., 'Management, Ideology and Practice', in Esland, G. and Salaman, G. (eds.), *The Politics of Work and Occupation* (Open University Press, Milton Keynes, 1980). pp. 279–302.
39. The reference here is to Mintzberg, H., *The Nature of Managerial Work* (Harper, New York, 1973).
40. For a review of this development see Bradley D., Walker, N. and Wilkie, R., *Managing the Police* (Wheatsheaf, Brighton, 1986), pp. 33–61.
41. Lilienfield, R., *The Rise of Systems Theory: An Ideological Analysis* (Wiley, New York, 1978). As Child puts it: 'The principal point of reference for contingency theory remains the same as that of earlier approaches, namely a logic of effectiveness'. Child, J., 'Organization: a Choice for Man', in Child, J. (ed.), *Man and Organization* (Allen and Unwin, London, 1973), pp. 234–58 (p. 238).
42. Stewart, R., 'Managerial Behaviour: How Research has Changed the Traditional Picture', in Earl, M.J. (ed.), *Perspectives in Management* (Oxford University Press, Oxford, 1983), pp. 82–98; Anthony, P.D., *The Foundation of Management* (Tavistock, London, 1986).
43. For general reviews of this literature see Mintzberg, H., op. cit., (1973); Storey, J., op. cit., (1983); Buckingham, J. and Lawrence, P., 'The Real Work of Managers', in Elliott, K. and Lawrence, P. (eds.), *Introducing Management* (Penguin, Harmondsworth, 1985), pp. 34–45; Watson, T., *Management Organization and Employment Strategy* (Routledge and Kegan Paul, London, 1986); and in particular Hales, C.P., 'What do Managers do? A Critical Review of the Evidence', *Journal of Management Studies*, vol. 23, (1986), pp. 88–115.
44. Carlson, S., *Executive Behaviour* (Strombergs, Stockholm, 1951).
45. Mintzberg, H., op. cit., (1973).
46. Hales, C.P., op. cit., (1986), p. 101.
47. For a theoretical justification and empirical elaboration of this view see Stewart, R., *Choices for the Manager* (McGraw-Hill, Maidenhead, 1982). A comparative analysis of this issue is to be found in Child, J. and Kieser, A., 'Organization and Managerial Roles in British and West German Companies: An Examination of the Culture-Free Thesis', in Lammers, C.J. and Hickson, D.J. (eds.), *Organizations Alike and Unlike: International and Inter-Institutional Studies in the Sociology of Organizations* (Routledge and Kegan Paul, London, 1979), pp. 251–71.
48. For an excellent example of a study that illustrates the schizoid character of managerial work see Fletcher, C., 'The End of Management', in Child, J., op. cit., (1973), pp. 135–57.
49. Hales, C.P., op. cit., (1986), p. 102.
50. For a development of this point see Mintzberg, H., 'The Manager's Job: Folklore and Fact', in Matteson, M.T. and Ivancevich, J.M. (eds.), *Management Classics* (Goodyear Publishing Corporation, California, 2nd edition, 1981), pp. 63–84.
51. Lindblom, C.E., 'The Science of Muddling Through', *Public Administration Review*, vol. 19, (1959), pp. 79–88.

52. Stewart, R., op. cit., (1983), p. 52.
53. Willmott, H., 'Studying Managerial Work: A Critique and a Proposal', *Journal of Management Studies*, vol. 24, (1987), pp. 249–70.
54. Gouldner, A., *Wildcat Strike* (Antioch Press, New York, 1954).
55. Dalton, M., *Men Who Manage* (Wiley, New York, 1959).
56. Burns, T. and Stalker, G.M., *The Management of Innovation* (Tavistock, London, 1961).
57. Sayles, L.R., *Managerial Behaviour: Administration in Complex Organizations* (McGraw-Hill, New York, 1964).
58. Pettigrew, A.N., *The Politics of Organizational Decision-Making* (Tavistock, London, 1973).
59. Kotter, J.P., *The General Managers* (Free Press, New York, 1982).
60. Cohen, A.P., *The Management of Myths* (Manchester University Press, Manchester, 1975); Gowler, D. and Legge, K., 'The Meaning of Management and the Management of Meaning: A View from Social Anthropology', in Earl, M.J., op. cit., (1983), pp. 197–233; Golding, D., 'Symbolism, Sovereignty and Domination in an Industrial Hierarchical Organization', *Sociological Review*, vol. 27, (1969), pp. 169–77; Pfeffer, J., 'Management as Symbolic Action: The Creation and Maintenance of Organizational Paradigms', in Cummings, L.L. and Stow, B. (eds.), *Research on Organizational Behaviour*, vol. 3 (J.A. Press, Greenwich, 1981); Roberts, J., 'The Moral Character of Management Practice', *Journal of Management Studies*, vol. 23, (1984), pp. 287–300; Lebas, M. and Weigenstein, J., 'Management Control: The Roles of Rules, Markets and Culture', *Journal of Management Studies*, vol. 23, (1986), pp. 259–73; Ray, C.A., 'Corporate Culture: The Last Frontier of Control', *Journal of Management Studies*, vol. 23, (1986), pp. 287–98; Daudi, P., *The Discourse of Power in Managerial Praxis* (Basil Blackwell, Oxford, 1986).
61. Gowler, D. and Legge, K., op. cit., (1983), p. 229. For an excellent case study illustration of this point see Roberts, J., op. cit., (1984).
62. Pettigrew, A., *The Awakening Giant: Continuity and Change in ICI* (Basil Blackwell, Oxford, 1985), p. 44.
63. For an empirical illustration of this point see Burns, T., *The BBC* (Macmillan, London, 1979).
64. Cohen provides some interesting material on the alternative strategies of myth management that managers have available in situations where social change threatens to undermine traditional cultural values. He distinguishes between cultural extension (demonstrating the consistency between new ideas and established values) and cultural substitution (fundamental transformation in political structures in order to generate values supportive of the new status quo). The latter, he argues, calls for a much more complex and painful programme of myth management. On these points see Cohen, A.P., op. cit., (1975), pp. 16–18.
65. Pettigrew's study of change in ICI provides an insightful example of this process and the dangers that it entails. See Pettigrew, A., op. cit., (1985).

66. Two recent popularisers of this view are Jay, A., *Management and Machiavelli* (Penguin, Harmondsworth, 1967) and Macoby, M., *The Gamesman: The New Corporate Leaders* (Simon and Schuster, New York, 1977).
67. Willmott, H., op. cit., (1987), p. 253.
68. Hales, C., op. cit., (1986), p. 111. Hales is also highly critical of the labour process theorists for not dealing adequately with the complexity of managerial behaviour in work.
69. Chapter six and the concluding section of this book will attend more closely to the moral implications of this de-contextualised view of managerial work.
70. Here, we are dealing with patterns of work behaviour and relations discovered among directors and senior managers in corporate hierarchies. The broader issue of the class location and role of the latter (as well as that of middle and first-line managers) is discussed in Chapter five.
71. Mace, M.L., *Directors: Myth and Reality* (Harvard Business School Press, Boston, Massachusetts, 1986), pp. 178–85.
72. Mangham, I.L., *Power and Performance in Organizations: An Exploration of Executive Process* (Basil Blackwell, Oxford, 1986), p. 64.
73. Burns, T. and Stalker, G.M., op. cit., (1961).
74. Ibid., p. 250.
75. Winkler, J.T., 'The ghost at the bargaining table: directors and industrial relations', *British Journal of Industrial Relations*, vol. 12, No. 2, (1974), pp. 191–212.
76. Pettigrew, A.M., op. cit., (1986).
77. Winkler suggests that this attitude can be explained in terms of a complex interaction between logical, ideological, political and preferential factors.
78. Pettigrew, A.M., op. cit., (1986), p. 461.
79. Pfeffer, J., *Power in Organizations* (Pitman, Boston, 1981), pp. 254–66.
80. Pahl, R.E. and Winkler, J.T., 'The Economic Elite: Theory and Practice', in Stanworth, P. and Giddens, A. (eds.), *Elites and Power in British Society* (Cambridge University Press, Cambridge, 1974), pp. 102–22.
81. Fidler, J., *The British Business Elite* (Routledge and Kegan Paul, London, 1981).
82. Scott, J., *Corporations, Classes and Capitalism* (Hutchinson, London, 2nd edition, 1985).
83. Pahl and Winkler further subdivide the operational category into non-executive, subsidiary and cabinet boards. They suggest that the latter sub-type is potentially the most complex – in terms of organisational politics – because there is no clear division between 'outside gatekeepers' and 'inside proposers' as there is in the other two sub-types. On this point see Pahl and Winkler, op. cit., (1974), p. 108.
84. Pahl and Winkler distinguish allocative and operational control in the following terms: 'control over the allocation process is analytically

and also very often empirically distinct from control over the day-to-day use of resources already allocated. . . . There will be overlap between the two forms, in the sense that some individuals will have both. There will be a reciprocal relationship between them, in the sense that a man starting with one form may acquire the other. There will be gradations in both forms of control, in the sense that for any company or group they may be divided among several people who will have more or less control. Nonetheless, it is important to keep the two forms of control conceptually distinct. The difference between them becomes clear when the providers of capital choose to withdraw it, leaving the users in very changed circumstances, at the extreme with nothing to operate at all'. Pahl and Winkler, op. cit., (1974), p. 114. This is clearly a central issue, which we shall pursue in greater detail in Chapter five.

85. Pahl and Winkler, op. cit., (1974), pp. 109–11.
86. Fidler provides a threefold categorisation of directors' social imagery, in terms of entrepreneurs, family businessmen and bureaucrats. On this point see Fidler, J., op. cit., (1981), p. 143.
87. Fidler, J., op. cit., (1981), p. 143. This closely parallels Nichols, T., *Ownership, Control and Ideology* (Allen and Unwin, London, 1969).
88. Scott, J., op. cit., (1985), pp. 179–80.
89. Whitley, R., 'Taking Firms Seriously as Economic Actors: Towards a Sociology of Firm Behaviour', *Organization Studies*, vol. 8, (1987), pp. 125–47.
90. Whitley refers to managerial rationalities as general belief systems, decision routines, calculating practices and cultural frameworks that provide a dominant coalition with an epistemology from which to design and implement organisational strategies. On this see Whitley, R., op. cit., (1987). For an empirical illustration of this concept see Gunz, H. and Whitley, R., 'Managerial Cultures and Industrial Strategies in British Firms', *Organization Studies*, vol. 6, (1985), pp. 247–73.
91. Whitley, R., op. cit., (1987), p. 143.
92. For numerous empirical illustrations of this point see Kotter, J.P., op. cit., (1982).
93. Bendix, R., op. cit., (1974), pp. 211–12.
94. Ibid., p. 233.
95. Littler, C.R., *The Development of the Labour Process in Capitalist Societies* (Heinemann, London, 1982), p. 88.
96. Gospel, H., 'The Development of Management Organization in Industrial Relations: A Historical Perspective', in Thurley, K. and Wood, S. (eds.), *Industrial Relations and Management Strategy* (Cambridge University Press, Cambridge, 1983), pp. 91–110.
97. Kay, E., *The Crisis in Middle Management* (American Management Association, New York, 1974).
98. Mintzberg, H., *The Structuring of Organizations* (Prentice-Hall, Englewood Cliffs, N.J., 1979). Mintzberg sees middle management as consisting of three distinct but interrelated groups – middle-line managers, technical analysts and support staff. This categorisation is

based on their organisational location and the specialised functional task that it requires. Middle-line managers directly supervise the performance of the operating core; technical analysts provide the information and advice on which line managers act; support staff are external to the operating work flow and provide the indirect services it requires.

99. Dalton, M., op. cit., (1959); Sayles, L., op. cit., (1964); Horne, J.H. and Lupton, T., 'The Work Activities of Middle Managers: An Exploratory Study', *Journal of Management Studies*, vol. 2, (1965), pp. 14–33; Sofer, C., *Men in Mid-Career: A Study of British Managers and Technical Specialists* (Cambridge University Press, Cambridge, 1970); Handy, C., *Understanding Organizations* (Penguin, Harmondsworth, 1976); Hill, S., *Competition and Control at Work* (Heinemann, London, 1981); Shorris, E., *The Oppressed Middle: Politics of Middle Management, Scenes from Corporate Life* (Anchor Press/Doubleday, New York, 1981); Lawrence, P.A., *Management in Action* (Routledge and Kegan Paul, London, 1984).

100. Fox, A., *A Sociology of Work in Industry* (Macmillan, London, 1971), p. 84.

101. Kay, E., op. cit., (1974).

102. Shorris, E., op. cit., (1981).

103. On this point see Fletcher, C., op. cit., (1973); Thomas, A.B., 'Managerial Careers and the Problem of Control', Paper to European Group on Organization Studies, *Conference on Capital and Control*, University of York, 1981; Ray, C.A., 'The Conceptual Deskilling and Reskilling of Line Managers', unpublished Paper, Sociology Board, Merrill College, University of California, 1985.

104. Chapter six pursues this theme in greater detail.

105. A more detailed justification of this prognosis is provided in Mills, C.W., *White Collar* (Oxford University Press, New York, 1951).

106. Armstrong. P., 'Competition Between Organizational Professions and the Evolution of Management Control Strategies', in Thompson, K. (ed.), *Work, Employment and Unemployment* (Open University Press, Milton Keynes, 1984), pp. 97–120; Armstrong, P., 'Management Control Strategies and Inter-Professional Competition: The Cases of Accountancy and Personnel Management', in Knights, D. and Willmott, H., op. cit., (1986), pp. 19–43; Child, J., 'New Technology and the Service Class', *Work Organization Research Centre Working Paper Series*, No. 6, University of Aston, 1985; Smith, C., *Technical Workers: Class, Labour and Trade Unionism* (Macmillan, London, 1987).

107. Armstrong has pointed out that this contrasts sharply with the position in West Germany. On this point see Armstrong, P., 'Engineers, Management and Trust', Paper to the *Organization and Control of the Labour Process Conference*, University of Manchester Institute of Science and Technology, 1986.

108. For an analysis of the symbolic functions of accountancy theory and practice see Earl, M.J., 'Accounting in Management', in Earl, M.J. (ed.), op. cit., (1983).

100   THE SOCIOLOGY OF MANAGEMENT

109. Armstrong, P., op. cit., (1984), p. 116.
110. Melling, J., 'Non-Commissioned Officers: British Employers and their Supervisory Workers 1880–1920', *Social History*, vol. 4, (1980), pp. 183–221.
111. Gospel, H., op. cit., (1983).
112. Littler, C.R., op. cit., (1982), pp. 86–7. Child and Partridge argue that the decline in the foreman's power and authority was somewhat uneven across British industry; in some sectors – such as construction – substantial vestiges of control still remained during the post-1945 era. On this issue see Child, J. and Partridge, B., *Lost Managers: Supervisors in Industry and Society* (Cambridge University Press, Cambridge, 1982).
113. Littler, C.R., op. cit., (1982), p. 87. Also on this point see Anthony, P.D., op. cit., (1986).
114. Gospel, H., op. cit., (1983), p. 99. Gospel argues that this process of managerial centralisation was related to factors such as the move to large-scale industrial organisation, increased administrative complexity and the demands made on management control structures by intensified international competitiveness in the market-place.
115. On this point see Ray, C.A., op. cit., (1985).
116. Of course, other developments also led to a decrease in the foreman's power and authority, such as the increasing power of trade unions as exemplified in the rise of the shop-steward movement.
117. Child, J. and Partridge, B., op. cit., (1982), p. 8.
118. Excellent reviews of these studies are to be found in Thurley, K. and Wirdenius, H., *Supervision: A Reappraisal* (Heinemann, London, 1973), pp. 1–24; Hirszowicz, M., *Industrial Sociology: An Introduction* (Martin Robertson, Oxford, 1981), pp. 98–124; Carter, B., *Capitalism, Class Conflict and the New Middle Class* (Routledge and Kegan Paul, London, 1985), pp. 114–23.
119. Hill, S., 'Supervisory Roles and the Man in the Middle: Dock Foremen', *British Journal of Sociology*, vol. 24, (1973), pp. 205–21.
120. Child, J. and Partridge, B., op. cit., (1982), pp. 191–218.
121. Ibid., p. 117. For a highly critical view of the 'man in the middle' thesis, see Fletcher, C., 'Man in the Middle: A Reformulation of the Thesis', *Sociological Review*, vol. 17, (1969), pp. 341–54.
122. Hill, S., op. cit., (1973).
123. Nichols, T. and Beynon, H., *Living With Capitalism: Class Relations and the Modern Factory* (Routledge and Kegan Paul, London, 1977), pp. 44–67.
124. Armstrong, P., 'Class Relations at the Point of Production: A Case Study', *Sociology*, vol. 17, (1983), pp. 339–58.
125. Rose, D., Marshall, G., Newby, H. and Vogler, C., 'Goodbye to Supervisors?', *Work, Employment and Society*, vol. 1, (1987), pp. 7–24.
126. Ibid., pp. 18–20.
127. Harris, R., *Power and Powerlessness in Industry: An Analysis of the Social Relations of Production* (Tavistock, London, 1987).
128. Rose, et al., op. cit., (1987), p. 22.

4

MANAGING CONFLICT

INTRODUCTION

The ubiquity of conflict within the practice of management has been implicit throughout the previous discussion. The purpose of this chapter is to subject the process of conflict management to systematic analysis and evaluation.

This analysis will be developed in the following way: first, a discussion of the sources of industrial conflict located within the employment relationship in capitalist work organisations; second, a review of the forms of social action through which these mainsprings of conflict are expressed; third, an assessment of the range of social practices and mechanisms that managers deploy to regulate conflict behaviour; fourth, an evaluation of the contribution – either intended or unintended – that these practices and mechanisms make to the generation of conflict within the employment relationship. A number of case studies will be briefly outlined with the objective of illustrating the general points made in preceding sections.

SOURCES OF CONFLICT

Two major sources of conflict inherent in the employment relationship have been identified by a number of industrial sociologists.[1] First, the fact that the employment relationship is an exchange relationship in which the rate at which wages are exchanged for labour is subject to opposing interests and priorities. Second, the fact that the employment relationship necessarily requires the subordination of the employee to the authority of the employer. Both of these mainsprings of industrial conflict reveal the fundamental character of employment within capitalist work organisations – that the employer purchases the employee's capacity to work (their 'labour power') but must exercise continuing control over the latter in order to ensure that this potential (their 'labour') is realised. As Brown puts it:

> There are therefore two sources of conflict inherent in the employer–employee relation: the conflicting interests over the rate of exchange of pay for work – wages and salaries are costs for the employer and income for the employees; and the conflicting interests over the exercise of authority by the employer – what is order and control for employers is loss of autonomy and constraint for employees.[2]

The economic, political and moral terms on which labour power is transformed into labour are subject to a continuing process of negotiation in which management attempts to control work performance through the design and implementation of administrative mechanisms directed at securing required effort levels from employees.[3] In turn, the forms of conflict regulation and control deployed by management are reciprocally linked to the modes of individual and collective action in which employees engage with the intention of avoiding, resisting and manipulating the effort levels managers are attempting to impose.

However, as Edwards[4] has argued, an analysis of the effort bargain has to be grounded in an appreciation of the production process. The latter provides the material conditions and social structures within which bargaining – over the economic terms on which wages are exchanged for effort and the organisational terms on which compliance is secured – takes place. As such, capitalist work organisations provide social arenas within which struggles over the terms on which production is carried out must be managed in order to ensure that continuous capital accumulation can be maintained. In this sense, exploitation and the structured antagonisms it generates stand at the analytical core of the employment relationship in that they provide the basic institutional parameters within which conflict is managed:

> Exploitation does not rest on the contingent fact that one
> group happens to be more powerful than another. It is in-
> herent in production relations . . . In exploitive production
> relations . . . a surplus is produced within social relations of
> dominance and subordination, and there is no sense in which
> the production of the surplus can be seen as a process in which
> the dominant and subordinate groups are in equivalent
> positions.[5]

Thus, the use of labour power under the direction of the employer within a production process geared to continuous capital
accumulation (through the imposition of a structure of domination)
is the analytical foundation for an understanding of industrial
conflict. It is management's job to ensure that labour power is
utilised in such a manner that profitable production can be sustained on a continuous basis. This requires the design, implementation and monitoring of a wide range of mechanisms aimed at
ensuring that the conflicts necessarily generated within the production process do not seriously threaten capital accumulation. These
mechanisms are likely to be reciprocally related to the forms of
worker recalcitrance experienced within particular work organisations. Their implementation will invariably produce new sources of
tension and conflict within the work organisation, and these are
likely to require – but may not get – innovative regulative practices
to cope with novel modes of resistance.

FORMS OF CONFLICT

The forms of social action through which industrial conflict can be
expressed have been identified in relation to three major analytical
considerations. First, the level of social organisation at which they
occur; second, the extent to which they entail concerted action
between a plurality of social actors; third, the nature of the issues to
which that action relates. Each of these considerations will be
discussed in turn with a view to providing a basis for assessing the
range of conflict-regulating mechanisms deployed by management
in the following section.

We can identify three levels of social organisation at which industrial conflict occurs: institutional, organisational and be-havioural.[6]

Institutional conflict refers to the broad pattern of social rela-tionships within a society over and through which dominant and subordinate groups struggle to impose their priorities on each other. Conflict over the macro-structure of social institutions through which productive activity is carried on has fundamental implications for the rest of society. It is, after all, interlocked with a wide range of institutional configurations concerned with domestic life, politics, culture and gender.[7] The institutional structure through which economic life is carried on provides a set of under-lying social principles and practices that will have fateful con-sequences both for the operation of individual productive units and the quality of working life made available within them.[8] If these principles are radically undermined through intense struggle and conflict, then it is probable that the domain assumptions underpin-ning other areas of social life will be affected far beyond the confines of the workplace. Conflict over the institutional structure of the economic system is likely to spill over into other areas of social life, although the extent to which this occurs is subject to considerable variation over time and place.

That set of institutions which comprises the mode of production within any society provides a framework of social relations and related social practices that organises producers and allocates the distribution of the surplus they produce. It provides a network of general principles and structural parameters within which primary producers and managerial practitioners interact at the level of work organisation. Organisational conflict concerns the specific mechan-isms through which dominant groups extract sufficient effort at the right rates of exchange from subordinate groups. These mechan-isms consist of a web of disciplinary practices that produce and reproduce the structure of workplace relations through which pro-duction is undertaken. They emerge from and generate particular patterns of conflict within the workplace in which managers and workers negotiate the frontier of control on the shop floor.[9]

Behavioural conflict manifests itself in the actual conduct of individuals and groups within the work organisation as they act to realise their interests in opposition to those pursued by others. The participants in this situation recognise and articulate a clash of interests that provides them with a rationale for action aimed at imposing their will on their opponents.[10] At this level, conflict is expressed in a social form characterised by a relatively high degree of social visibility and directness.

The relationship between each of these levels of conflict is not one in which patterns at a lower level can be read off from those operating at a higher level. As we saw in our earlier discussion of levels of control,[11] there is a loose coupling between each of the levels, such that higher levels of conflict provide broad constraints within which lower-level developments occur. But there is no sense in which we can assume that patterns of conflict emerging at the organisational or behavioural levels can be determined by structural imperatives operating at the institutional level.[12]

Discussion of the comparative social cohesiveness and complexity of different types of industrial conflict has usually focused on the distinction between collective, or organised, conflict on the one hand and individual, or unorganised, conflict on the other.[13] The first – as exemplified in strikes, working to rule, lock-outs and output restriction – is deemed to involve relatively large numbers of people acting on the basis of a strategic assessment of the deprivations they face and a rational plan of action to remove them. It is characterised by a relatively high degree of social cohesion and control both as to strategic ends and tactical means. Individual conflict, on the other hand – as exemplified in absenteeism, labour turnover, sabotage and accidents – is assumed to be characterised by randomness as to objectives, and fragmentation as to means. Highly individualised and unco-ordinated in nature, this sort of conflict is treated as a spontaneous and immediate response to perceived deprivations. It is dominated by short-term tactical objectives and symbolic gestures of rejection.[14] Conspicuous by its absence is the degree of rational planning and control associated with collective forms of conflict.

Each of these types of conflict is thought to require an appropriate regulative response from management. Collective/organised conflict is deemed to elicit a mode of regulation focused on the institutionalisation of opposing interests and the constraints that this imposes on patterns of conflict that emerge at the organisational or behavioural levels. Individual/unorganised conflict produces a regulative response based on the development and manipulation of informal or unofficial practices that contain the problems that it poses for continuity of production.

These regulative modes – and the interaction between them – will be discussed in greater detail in the following section. However, it is important to note that this distinction between different types of conflict, and the regulative patterns associated with them, is best thought of as a continuum in which different forms shade into each other and change over time. Within work organisations, a range of conflict patterns and regulative frameworks are likely to evolve and develop over time as both management and workers respond to (or anticipate) changes to the external context in which they operate. Consequently, managers are likely to draw on a multiplicity of regulative strategies and structures, although certain patterns may well dominate for a period of time.

The issues underlying industrial conflict – at whatever level or in whatever form they occur – have been classified in a number of different ways.[15] We can distinguish between control issues, reward issues and moral issues – although any particular example of industrial conflict is likely to contain elements of all three types. Control issues are concerned with disputes over the power – that is, the capacity – to determine the organisational structures in which production processes will function. They focus upon the organisational resources and assets through which co-ordinated productive activity is made possible. Reward issues are centred upon disagreements over the distribution and allocation of economic and symbolic remuneration attached to different positions within the social structure of the work organisation. Moral issues highlight disputes over the legitimacy of claims attached to the status and exercise of rights as entitlements to certain kinds of preferment or consideration in decision-making over the allocation and distribution of organisational assets. They focus on the moral order that underpins the organisation of productive activity within economic enterprises.[16]

Conventionally, it is assumed that conflict over the allocation and distribution of material rewards is the dominant factor in accounting for the largest empirical range and variation of industrial disputes.[17] However, this view has been challenged in recent years both in relation to its empirical veracity and its theoretical adequacy regarding a more sophisticated view of industrial conflict as a multifaceted and complex social phenomenon.[18] In particular, the failure to give sufficient analytical and empirical weight to the underlying power struggle between dominant and subordinate groups, which provides the social foundations of productive activity in capitalist modes of production, is seen as a major limitation stemming from the economistic view.[19]

This survey of the forms of social action that articulate the underlying sources of conflict embedded within the employment relationship – in terms of levels, complexity and issues – provides the analytical base for an assessment of the modes of conflict regulation utilised by management in the following section.

MODES OF CONFLICT REGULATION

Debate over the management of industrial conflict has been dominated by the institutionalisation thesis. This has been so whether at the level of general institutional structures or at the level of individual companies and workplaces.[20] Within the latter, attention has been focused upon the development of an internal state constituted by a formalised collective bargaining system, codified collective agreements, written disciplinary procedures and internally managed labour markets.[21] At the macro-level, discussion has centred upon the development of structural mechanisms within the political economies of advanced capitalist societies that lead to an institutional separation between industrial conflict on the one hand and class conflict on the other.[22] These two levels of analysis converge in the form of an evolutionary theory that predicts the eventual depoliticisation of industrial conflict as a result of the increasing maturity of regulative mechanisms within the factory, company and industrial relations system at large.[23] Initially, we shall analyse the general thesis before proceeding to an exposition of micro-level trends.

One of the clearest expressions of the institutionalisation thesis is provided by Dahrendorf:

> in post-capitalist society, industry and society have, by contrast to capitalist society, been dissociated. Increasingly, the social relations of industry, including industrial conflict, do not dominate the whole of society but remain confined in their patterns and problems to the sphere of industry. Industry and industrial conflict are, in post-capitalist society, institutionally isolated, i.e., confined within the borders of that proper realm and robbed of their influence on other spheres of society . . .

industrial conflict increasingly becomes *industrial* conflict without reference to general social and political problems . . . the intensity of industrial conflict has decreased also. . . . Above all, in contemporary societies industrial conflict and political conflict are no longer identical.[24]

Dahrendorf points to a number of interrelated institutional developments that have produced this situation. They include the integration of trade unions within the collective bargaining process, the evolution of sophisticated mechanisms of consultation, mediation and arbitration, the separation between professional management and private owners, and the overall bureaucratisation of the industrial organisation. These are seen to result in a sharp reduction in the intensity of industrial conflict and the structural containment of the frictional tensions that remain within the industrial sphere:

> The protagonists, issues, and patterns of industrial conflict have been severed from the antagonisms that divide political society; it is carried on in relative isolation. . . . Diminishing intensity and violence of conflict have their effect on the modes of structure change in industry. They would suggest that sudden as well as radical changes are largely absent on the contemporary scene. Changes of conditions and structures occur gradually and remain piecemeal.[25]

This view was echoed by writers such as Ross and Hartman,[26] and Kerr,[27] who anticipated a substantial reduction in the range and intensity of industrial conflict – particularly over the readiness to use the strike weapon – as a result of the evolution of more effective institutional mechanisms of conflict containment and control. In particular, the increasing scope, maturity and resilience of collective bargaining processes were seen to provide management with a network of rules that would tie workers and their representatives into a normative order from which they could not – and would not wish to – escape. This normative order would automatically filter out demands and conduct that were seen to threaten the status quo, while at the same time providing a forum in which conflict could be channelled within acceptable institutional limits.

Those conflicts that did remain would take on a more co-ordinated and routinised quality in which the institutional needs of the trade unions for stable and bureaucratised procedures facilitated a more rational appreciation of attainable organisational goals. This was paralled by a growing economism on the part of rank and file workers and trade union negotiators in which the ideological polarisations characteristic of traditional working class communities were superseded by the instrumentalism of the new middle class.[28] Uninterested in the mechanisms through which work was organised and managed, this latter group – numerically and politically dominant in all industrial capitalist societies – had reinforced the natural tendency on the part of trade union negotiators to focus on economic issues to the virtual exclusion of any interest in control issues. While distributive conflicts over the apportionment of economic surpluses were not ruled out – indeed, they were assumed to become the predominant issue informing the bargaining process – allocative conflicts over the ownership and control of productive resources were predicted to decline to the point of virtual extinction.[29]

Similar trends were seen to be operating at the micro-level in a number of industrial capitalist societies after World War II.[30] In Britain, a number of studies identified a general movement away from the indirect and fragmented methods of conflict regulation characteristic of the 1940s and 1950s towards a more formalised and integrated approach at plant and company levels in the 1960s and 1970s.[31] The bureaucratisation of plant-level bargaining, the move towards corporate-level wage negotiations and the development of standardised disputes procedures were seen as incremental components of an overall movement aimed at incorporating trade unions more effectively within the internal state.[32] In turn, it was envisaged that institutional developments such as these would contain industrial conflict within formal structures, significantly reducing the incidence and impact of anarchical sectional disputes.[33]

The institutionalisation of industrial conflict at workplace and company levels was also informed by a strategic objective close to the heart of many managers – discovering a new ideological foundation for the exercise of managerial power and control in a situation where old legitimations had become obsolete.[34] This problem was regarded as being particularly acute in an industrial relations system where management had proved to be consistently unable and/or unwilling to provide the direct leadership and support necessary to administer conflict in such a way that it did not threaten the existing distribution of power within industry.[35] While there is some evidence to suggest that British workers are prepared to recognise the legitimacy of formal regulative systems to a greater extent than some of their European counterparts,[36] this has never been regarded as sufficient in itself to guarantee the social legitimacy of managerial power. Indeed, the grudging acceptance of the latter by subordinate groups[37] has always been subject to the disruptive impact of wider socio-economic change on the effectiveness of existing regulative arrangements and the balance of power within industry. The conditional acceptance of existing regulative mechanisms by subordinate groups has required supplementation by a range of informal practices and understandings that bolster institutionalised relationships.

Consequently, the manufacture of consent on the shop floor has demanded the skilful deployment of informal norms, rules and relationships through which managers can negotiate and maintain workplace order. The role of management in initiating and sustaining an extensive network of informal practices through which conflict can be contained and controlled has been revealed by a number of empirical studies.[38] Rather than viewing custom and practice solely as a set of understandings that workers develop and defend, these studies have shown how managers manipulate the former to realise their own regulative objectives within the workplace. Thus, informal regulative mechanisms – the unwritten rules of work – may be relied on by management either as a supplement or alternative to more formalised arrangements aimed at incorporating workers and their shop-floor representatives within a bureaucratised control system.[39] Tacitly agreed arrangements, subject to renegotiation, may be more effective from management's point of view in providing the flexibility and adaptability it needs.

As Thompson notes, these informal regulative mechanisms often have the effect of 'transforming and redistributing management–worker conflicts into intra-employee competition'.[40] This diffuses structural conflict between management and workers inherent in the employment relationship into a series of sectionally based group conflicts in which work groups located in different parts of the production process are likely to see each other as obstacles to the realisation of their interests. In this way, it may be possible for management to minimise – if not prevent – the crystallisation of a collective consciousness and organisation on the part of shop-floor employees. As a result, the presentation of an individualist ideology among the workforce will contain – if not choke off – any embryonic developments in the direction of a collectivist consciousness and organisation with the potential to challenge managerial control.[41]

Nevertheless, there may be – and often is – a price to be paid for the pursuit of an effective regulative strategy of this kind. This is to be found in the preponderance of unorganised forms of conflict in work organisations where management have followed a regulative strategy aimed at dividing and isolating workers from each other. This may be as, if not more, difficult to manage than organised forms of conflict, which are more susceptible to formalised regulation mechanisms than patterns of conflict dominated by militant individualism – where workers mount isolated and randomised challenges to managerial control[42] – and the severe fragmentation this can produce.

However, management may be prepared to accept the costs – both economic and political – incurred in a conflict profile dominated by the unorganised type, given prevailing economic, technological and market conditions. If the latter change in such a way that these costs become increasingly painful to bear, then a movement towards greater formalisation and a more collectivised conflict pattern may be pursued.[43] On the other hand, institutionalisation at company and plant levels may produce unintended consequences for management in terms of the emergence of new conflict patterns that they had been unwilling and/or unable to contemplate.

It is to the latter – that is, to the role of management in generating conflict within the employment relationship and capitalist work organisations – that we must now turn.

MODES OF CONFLICT GENERATION

The contribution that institutionalisation – at whatever level or in whatever form it is followed – can make to the reinforcement of existing forms of conflict and the production of novel patterns has been displayed by a number of research studies.[44] They have also revealed the interest managers have in initiating and sustaining conflict situations – whether of an individualised or collectivised type – if this suits their purpose at a particular point in time.[45] As Batstone, *et al.* remind us:

Management may not want production at a *particular* time. They may be seeking an excuse for interruptions to production, and to avoid or alleviate the costs associated with such interruptions.[46]

In this sense, the conflict-producing consequences of the regulative mechanisms used by management are evident both in formal and informal control practices. As Armstrong and Goodman note in relation to the latter:

> Just as workers' custom and practice supplants or re-interprets some of the formal rules which govern the expectations which managers have of the workforce, so the C & P of managers or supervisors may supplant or re-interpret the formal rules governing the expectations which workers have of management. If workers' C & P constitutes an incursion into managerial prerogatives, so the C & P of managers and supervisors may constitute an incursion into workers' rights . . . whereas workers' C & P exists when the balance of power favours workers, managerial and supervisory C & P are dependent on a balance of power which favours management.[47]

The above view also highlights the close interaction between formal and informal regulative modes within management practice. This is true to the extent that it links developments in conflict patterns to the changing balance of power – or frontier of control – between management and workers on the shop floor and within the wider institutional context in which their representative organisations interact.

Evidence for the conflict-generating capacity of formalisation processes at company and workplace levels is provided by Turner, *et al.*,[48] and Batstone.[49] On the basis of their survey of 45 enterprises in Britain, the former conclude that:

> the consequent 'standardization' and 'formalization' of procedures in management generally or in labour relations, implies also a bureaucratization and increased rigidity that goes with a higher, rather than a lower, strike incidence.[50]

This seems to suggest that the greater the extent to which management relies on a process of formal routinisation for dealing with conflict, the more likely it is to lose the flexibility and adaptability associated with customary practices. As such, formal regulation and informal containment may need to be combined in such a way that an excessive reliance on formal methods – producing an intensification of organised conflict – can be avoided. In other words, there is a trade off between formalisation and informalisation, the terms of which may alter as the power relationship between management and unions changes. The problem for management is to ensure that the balance between formal modes and informal practices is appropriate to the situation they face, given that the latter is always likely the change in a way that will disturb the former.

Batstone's research on the post-Donovan situation in workplace industrial relations also reveals the conflict-generating consequences of formalisation in some detail:

> agreements could in fact reduce rather than increase managerial prerogative . . . the explicit statement of rules increased their visibility: it was now easier for groups to challenge management actions which were not consistent with the rules . . . rules are general by their very nature but have to be applied to specific situations. This provides considerable scope for negotiation over which rules should be applied . . . and their precise interpretation. . . . This point is particularly important where the new 'formal' rules are introduced into a situation previously governed by a complex of understandings, custom and practice and ad hoc rules . . . new 'formal' rules do not exist in a vacuum: they have to be applied to ongoing social situations which are characterized to varying degrees by understandings about 'the normal way of doing things'. To the extent that the new rules challenge these conventions, then far from leading to a new 'normative order' they may foster the very situation they were designed to avoid – some form of anomie.[51]

In addition to identifying these detailed problems of effectively implementing more formal conflict-regulating mechanisms on the shop floor, Batstone's research also shows how the attempt to bureaucratise workplace industrial relations produced consequences diametrically opposed to those intended. Thus, the strategy of formalising the informal system of shop-floor industrial relations (through corporate-level bargaining and factory-level collective agreement)[52] provided a new and powerful source of leverage that workers would use to challenge management's attempts to realise detailed control over labour utilisation in the workplace. The techniques that management relied on to secure the latter – such as productivity bargaining and job evaluation – were open to manipulation by workers in their attempt to resist the extension of formal control. Consequently, they became focal points for individual and collective conflict over the reasonableness displayed in their implementation and the legitimacy underlying their design. Far from constituting an extension of technical rationality in the social organisation of production – where conflicting sectional ends are subordinated to more efficient and effective technical means – both the strategy of formalisation and the specific mechanisms chosen to achieve it are sucked into a struggle for control.

Informal regulative mechanisms also have their problems. An excessive reliance on practices that re-interpret or supplant formal regulative controls may so thoroughly undermine and erode the authority of the latter that they lose all operational and ideological significance. This is likely to lead to a situation in which formalised management control systems and the long-term policy objectives to which they are directed become assimilated within workplace power struggles in which sectional interests and short-term tactical advantage are the overriding consideration.[53] The more well-developed and organised informal custom and practice rules become within the workplace, the easier it is for workers to challenge managerial control and constrain the operation of formal regulative mechanisms. While informal methods are useful – indeed necessary – adjuncts to formal managerial controls in many situations, they are always a double-edged weapon to the extent that they can be manipulated by workers in such a way that the latter's conflict-regulating capacity is effectively emasculated.[54] Disputes over issues that may once have been the preserve of formal allocative mechanisms – such as overtime rates, manning levels, line speeds and disciplinary infringements – can be transposed into a highly fragmented power bargaining context dominated by poorly regulated group or individual conflicts.[55]

The legitimatory problems that this process of deregulation can pose for management may be as, if not more, significant than its operational headaches. The ideology of managerial prerogative[56] – the right to manage – and of profitability as the underlying principle of efficient productive activity receive considerable institutional support and sustenance from formal regulative rule systems in which workers and managers are intermeshed.[57] If these systems are radically undermined as the result of management allowing – or being forced to concede – a degree of reliance on informal regulative practices that subverts the logic of formal controls, then these legitimising principles may be seriously damaged. At the very least, the reproduction of consent on the shop floor can become much more problematic for management in a situation where the struggle for workplace control has assumed an ideological intensity and organisational strength that cannot be effectively contained within formalised relationships and the legitimising principles they enshrine.[58]

CASE STUDIES IN CONFLICT MANAGEMENT

Let us now briefly review three case studies so that we can illuminate the three general themes that have emerged from the previous discussion. First, Friedman and Meredeen's[59] study of industrial conflict at the Ford Motor Company will be discussed with a view to illustrating the inherent limitations and contradictions of formalisation as a conventional mode of conflict regulation. Second, a selective exposition of research by Edwards and Scullion[60] on workplace industrial conflict will focus on the crucial significance of the interaction between formal and informal regulative practices in maintaining shop floor order. Third, the series of case studies on the initiation of worker participation schemes in a number of Scottish companies conducted by Cressey, MacInnes and Eldridge,[61] and highlighting the strategic importance of maintaining the ideological foundations of managerial power during and after the implementation of new modes of conflict regulation.

Friedman and Meredeen argue that the Ford industrial creed set out 'a strategy of tight labour management, spelled out in a detailed set of administrative procedures'.[62] This overriding emphasis on formal regulative mechanisms was evident at all managerial levels, stretching from first-line management on the production track to senior personnel professionals located at company headquarters. The long-term objective underlying this strategy of formalisation – which anticipated the Donovan Report's recommendations for greater standardisation and formalisation of workplace industrial relations by four years – was to enmesh the unions with a framework of bureaucratic controls facilitating predictability and stability in every aspect of the company's industrial relations. Adherence to formal procedures and institutions was elevated into an article of managerial faith that provided the operational and ideological foundations for management's industrial relations strategy.[63]

However, there had been no attempt to re-examine and re-evaluate this overwhelming reliance on formal regulative mechanisms in the light of fundamental changes to the political realities of shop-floor union power taking place in the company during the 1960s. The success of the strategy depended on management's ability to involve workplace trade union leaders in further institutionalisation of industrial conflict – through the incremental extension of joint-consultation committees and shop-floor bargaining procedures – at a time when the latter were most inclined and able to resist these advances. Not only this, but the attempt to instigate more accommodative practices of conflict management at workplace level was implemented through a strategy of formalisation that did not sufficiently appreciate the depth and intensity of sectional conflicts on the shop floor.

As a result, an unthinking acceptance of and perseverance with a formalistic strategy of conflict regulation by Ford management exacerbated shop-floor disputes. This was true to the extent that a highly bureaucratised system of conflict regulation at all organisational levels effectively excluded a number of sectional interests from real participation within the representative system.[64] At the same time, it provided work groups strategically located within the production system, and capable of using the potential power that it provided, with an institutional resource that they would turn to their own advantage. Both of these groups would use the formal machinery to good effect in the unstable conditions characteristic of the 1960s.

The research by Edwards and Scullion on patterns of workplace industrial conflict in seven British factories reveals the variety of formal and informal regulative mechanisms that management rely on to achieve shop-floor order and control. A number of their case studies illustrate the destabilising impact of rationalising strategies aimed at containing disputes over new working practices within formal institutional arrangements. This was particularly true in plants that had a strong tradition of shop-steward involvement in production planning and where the latter interpreted managerial actions aimed at placing industrial relations on a more formal and rational basis as a concerted campaign to undermine their authority.[65] The conflicts generated as a result of this clash of logics also revealed the range of informal sanctions and controls – such as stopping pay, cutting overtime and closure threats – which management had at their disposal to resolve disputes on terms acceptable to them.

However, an overriding commitment to formal regulative modes often prevented management from effectively deploying informal measures in order to overcome shop-floor resistance to change in working practices. The need to deploy a balanced package of methods focused on strategic objectives, and the tactical manoeuvres required to realise them, was often lost in a miasma of unplanned and contradictory responses to events as they spiralled out of control. The obsession with formalisation often excluded the sophisticated use of informal practices that would have coped with the threats the former posed to the existing framework of shop-floor order and control.

The research carried out by Cressey, MacInnes and Eldridge also brings out the co-existence of multiple systems of conflict regulation within work organisations and the problems this creates for management. Their series of case studies on the effectiveness of new participation structures and philosophies introduced by management in a number of Scottish companies displayed the broad mix of objectives and methods underlying these programmes. These ranged from developing a more planned response to the instabilities generated by multi-union collective bargaining structures to implementing more participative and efficient methods of quality control on the shop floor.

However, a long-term interest in maintaining the institutional and ideological foundations of managerial power was a common theme in all of the case studies. The institutional innovations that the latter trace were all informed by senior management's search for adequate forms of legitimation in conditions where existing modes of conflict regulation were under threat from instability, change and turbulence in the socio-economic environment:

Managers' interest in participation strategies springs directly

from this problem of consent and co-ordination that is at the
heart of the 'management' job. Managers have increasingly
had to take on board the solving of the social problems of
production. In so doing they have a far greater 'ideological'
and social role to play in the organization and its production
process. . . . Participation strategies and consultation were
setting down legitimate roles for the actors, boundaries for
responsibilities, validity of expertise and a form of relationship based on consent. Even though it appeared that the
consultation was doing little on the surface, its latent functions
were enabling the equilibrium to be sustained, largely in
management's favour.[66]

Yet there were definite limits on management's capacity to
manipulate perticipative structures to its own ideological and political advantage. Indeed, institutional innovations of this kind revealed the underlying reality of management practice as a fragile
process uniting conflicting demands and pressures within the enterprise through the use of participative mechanisms that are likely to
cause as many problems as they solve. The reality of managing
participative reforms emerging from this research is one of a process
characterised by deep-seated uncertainty and indeterminacy in
which the regulation of power conflicts over organisational ends
and means is the central feature.

CONCLUSION

This chapter has analysed the major forms of conflict regulation
practised by management within capitalist work organisations. It
has served to support the general picture of management practice
painted in previous chapters; that is, as a contradictory process in
which the structural constraints and conflicts inherent in managerial
conduct are endemic to the institutional framework through which
it is performed.

However, the sources of social conflict in the class structures of
advanced capitalist societies have not been examined in sufficient
detail and depth. It is to the location and function of management
within these class structures that we now turn.

REFERENCES

1. Brown, R.K., 'Sociologists and Industry: In Search of a Distinctive Competence', *Sociological Review*, vol. 29, (1981), pp. 217–35; Hill, S., *Competition and Control at Work* (Heinemann, London, 1981); Keenoy, T., *Invitation to Industrial Relations* (Basil Blackwell, Oxford, 1985); Edwards, P.K., *Conflict at Work: A Materialist Analysis of Workplace Relations* (Basil Blackwell, Oxford, 1986).
2. Brown, R.K., op. cit., (1981), p. 226.
3. Baldamus, G., *Efficiency and Effort* (Tavistock, London, 1961).
4. Edwards, P.K., op. cit., (1986).
5. Ibid., p. 66.
6. This section draws on Fox, A., *A Sociology of Work in Industry* (Macmillan, London, 1971); Sofer, C., *Organizations in Theory and Practice* (Heinemann, London, 1972); Pondy, C., 'Organizational Conflicts: Concepts and Models', in Thomas, J.M. and Bennis, W.G., (eds.), *Management of Change and Conflict* (Penguin, Harmondsworth, 1972), pp. 359–80; Edwards, P.K. and Scullion, H., *The Social Organization of Industrial Conflict* (Basil Blackwell, Oxford, 1982a).
7. The institutional centrality of work is discussed further in Brown, R.K., 'Work', in Abrams, P. and Brown, R.K. (eds.), *UK Society* (Weidenfeld and Nicholson, London, 1984), pp. 129–97.
8. For a particularly strong version of the view that basic economic structures tightly constrain work organisations see Ackroyd, A., Burrell, G., Hughes, M. and Whitaker, A., 'The Japanization of British Industry?', Paper presented to Conference on 'Japanization of British Industry', University of Wales Institute of Science and Technology, September 1987.
9. For an extended interpretation of this proposition see Edwards, P.K. and Scullion, H., 'Deviancy Theory and Industrial Praxis: A Study of Discipline and Social Control in an Industrial Setting', *Sociology*, vol. 16, No. 3, (1982b), pp. 322–39.
10. For a penetrating analysis of the concept of interests see Hindess, B., 'Interests in Political Analysis', in Law, J. (ed.), *Power, Action and Belief*, Sociological Review Monograph 32 (Routledge and Kegan Paul, London, 1986), pp. 112–31. This issue will be discussed at greater length in the following chapter.
11. See Chapter two.
12. Indeed, as Edwards points out, the logic of explanation can run in the opposite direction – from the behavioural and organisational conflict to wider forms of class conflict located at the institutional level. On this point see Edwards, P.K., op. cit., (1986).
13. For general reviews of this distinction see Kornhauser, A., Dubin, R. and Ross, A. (eds.), *Industrial Conflict* (McGraw-Hill, New York, 1954); Hyman, R., *Strikes* (Fontana, Glasgow, 3rd edition, 1984); Jackson, M., *Strikes: Industrial Conflict in Britain, USA and Australia* (Wheatsheaf Books, Sussex, 1987).

14. Hyman suggests that the distinction between organised and unorganised conflict is best regarded as a continuum of forms rather than an ideal-type dichotomy. On this point see Hyman, R., op. cit., (1984).
15. For example see Knowles, K.G., *Strikes: A Study in Industrial Conflict* (Basil Blackwell, Oxford, 1952); Turner, H.A., Clack, G. and Roberts, G., *Labour Relations in the Motor Industry* (Allen and Unwin, London, 1967); Eldridge, J.E.T., *Industrial Disputes: Essays in the Sociology of Industrial Relations* (Routledge and Kegan Paul, London, 1968); Batstone, E., Boraston, I. and Frenkel, S., *The Social Organization of Strikes* (Basil Blackwell, Oxford, 1978); Jackson, M., op. cit., (1987).
16. On the significance of moral issues for an understanding of industrial conflict see Macfarlane, L.J., *The Right to Strike* (Penguin, Harmondsworth, 1981).
17. For an elaboration of this point see Jackson, M., op. cit., (1987).
18. Gouldner's study of the violation of the indulgency pattern by management, the moral condemnation this provoked among workers and the economic conflicts it generated is a classic illustration of this point. On this see Chapter two.
19. Arguments supporting this view are to be found in Fox, A., *Beyond Contract: Work, Power and Trust Relations* (Faber and Faber, London, 1974); and Cronin, J.E., *Industrial Conflict in Modern Britain* (Croom Helm, London, 1979).
20. General reviews of the institutionalisation thesis are to be found in Hyman, op. cit., (1984); and Watson, T., *Sociology, Work and Industry* (Routledge and Kegan Paul, 2nd edition, London, 1987).
21. The concept of the internal state is developed in Burawoy, M., *The Politics of Production* (Verso, London, 1985).
22. Dahrendorf, R., *Class and Class Conflict in Industrial Society* (Routledge and Kegan Paul, London, 1959).
23. Ingham, G.K., *Strikes and Industrial Conflict: Britain and Scandinavia* (Macmillan, London, 1974); Jackson, M., op. cit., (1987).
24. Dahrendorf, R., op. cit., (1959), pp. 268–77.
25. Ibid., pp. 277–8.
26. Ross, A.M. and Hartman, P.T., *Changing Patterns of Industrial Conflict* (John Wiley, New York, 1960).
27. Kerr, C., Dunlop, J.T., Harbison, J.T. and Myers, C.A., *Industrialism and Industrial Man* (Harvard University Press, Cambridge, Mass., 1960).
28. For a review of the embourgeoisement thesis see Hirszowicz, M., *Industrial Sociology* (Martin Robertson, Oxford, 1981), pp. 141–71.
29. As Kerr, *et al.* so graphically expressed it: 'Persuasion, pressure and manipulation will take the place of the face-to-face combat of an earlier age. The battles will be in the corridors instead of the streets, and memos will flow instead of blood. . . . The great battles over conflicting manifestos will be replaced by a myriad of minor contests over comparative details'. (Kerr, C., *et al.*, *Industrialism and Industrial Man* (Penguin, Harmondsworth, 1973), pp. 273–4.

30. For a general overview of these developments see Barkin, S. (ed.), *Worker Militancy: Its Consequences* (Praeger, New York, 2nd edition, 1983).

31. Storey, J., *The Challenge to Management Control* (Hutchinson, London, 1981); Brown, W. (ed.), *The Changing Contours of British Industrial Relations* (Basil Blackwell, Oxford, 1981); Daniel, W.W. and Millward, N., *Workplace Industrial Relations in Britain* (Heinemann, London, 1983); Poole, M. (ed.), *Industrial Relations in the Future* (Routledge and Kegan Paul, London, 1984); Terry, M., 'Shop Steward Development and Management Strategies', in Bain, G.S. (ed.), *Industrial Relations in Britain* (Basil Blackwell, Oxford, 1983), pp. 67–91; Purcell, J. and Sisson, K., 'Strategies and Practice in the Management of Industrial Relations', in Bain (ed.), op. cit., (1983), pp. 95–120.

32. For a general review and assessment of the proposition that shop stewards were being incorporated into management control systems in the 1970s see Batstone, E., *Working Order: Workplace Industrial Relations in Britain Over Two Decades* (Basil Blackwell, Oxford, 1984); and 'Bureaucracy, Oligarchy and Incorporation in Shop Steward Organizations in the 1980s', in Jacobi, O., Jessop, B., Kastendich, H. and Regini, M. (eds.), *Technological Change, Rationalization and Industrial Relations* (Croom Helm, London, 1986), pp. 137–60.

33. For an assessment of the Donovan Report's prescriptions for institutional reform of workplace industrial relations see Batstone, E., op. cit., (1984).

34. For a review of the ideological context in which the re-institutionalisation of workplace conflict was recommended as a policy for restoring managerial authority see Goldthorpe, J.H., 'Industrial Relations in Great Britain: A Critique of Reformism', in Clarke, T. and Clements, L. (eds.), *Trade Unions Under Capitalism* (Fontana, Glasgow, 1977), pp. 184–224.

35. For an assessment of the long-term historical perspective in which the failure of British management to engage with labour in a direct and effective fashion needs to be evaluated, see Fox, A., *History and Heritage: The Social Origins of the British Industrial Relations System* (Allen and Unwin, London, 1985); and Anthony, P.D., *The Foundations of Management* (Tavistock, London, 1986).

36. Gallie, D., *In Search of the New Working Class* (Cambridge University Press, Cambridge, 1978). For a rather different view comparing workers' relative acceptance of management control systems in Britain and Germany – as opposed to Britain and France as in Gallie's study – see Maitland, I., *The Causes of Industrial Disorder* (Routledge and Kegan Paul, London, 1983).

37. For an elaboration of this point see Parkin, F., *Class Inequality and Political Order* (McGibbon and Kee, London, 1971).

38. Roy, D.F., 'Efficiency and "The Fix": Informal Intergroup Relations in a Piecework Machine Shop', *American Sociological Review*, vol. 18, (1953), pp. 507–14; Lupton, T., *On the Shop Floor* (Pergamon,

Oxford, 1963); Terry, M., 'The Inevitable Growth of Informality', *British Journal of Industrial Relations*, vol. 15, (1977), pp. 76–90; Burawoy, M., *Manufacturing Consent: Changes in the Labour Process under Monopoly Capitalism* (University of Chicago Press, Chicago, 1979); Armstrong, P. and Goodman, J.F., 'Managerial and Supervisory Custom and Practice', *Industrial Relations Journal*, vol. 10, (1979), pp. 12–24.

39. For a number of examples of this see Edwards, P.K., op. cit., (1986).
40. Thompson, P., *The Nature of Work* (Macmillan, London, 1983), p. 161. For an attempt to provide empirical documentation of this practice in one plant see Thompson, P. and Bannon, E., *Working the System: The Shop Floor and New Technology* (Pluto Press, London, 1985).
41. For an excellent empirical illustration of this point see Cunnison, S., *Wages and Work Allocation* (Tavistock, London, 1966).
42. See Edwards, P.K., op. cit., (1986), for an extended discussion of militant individualism.
43. Specific examples of this are to be found in Edwards, P.K. and Scullion, H., op. cit., (1982a).
44. Turner, H.A., Roberts, G. and Roberts, D., *Management Characteristics and Labour Conflict* (Cambridge University Press, Cambridge, 1974); Batstone, E. op. cit., (1984).
45. Examples of this are to be found in Beynon, H., *Working for Ford* (Penguin, Harmondsworth, 1973).
46. Batstone, E., *et al.*, op. cit., (1978), pp. 36–7.
47. Armstrong, P. and Goodman, J.F., op. cit., (1979), pp. 14–23.
48. Turner, H., *et al.*, op. cit., (1967).
49. Batstone, E., op. cit., (1984).
50. Turner, H., *et al.*, op. cit., (1967), p. 74.
51. Batstone, E., op. cit., (1984), p. 298.
52. Both of these institutional reforms were central components of the reform strategy proposed by the Donovan Report, which is analysed in some detail in Crouch, C., *Class Conflict and the Industrial Relations Crisis* (Heinemann, London, 1974).
53. This can also cause serious managerial problems for trade union bureaucracies in their search to maintain and enhance organisational strength above plant level. For an extended discussion of the institutional needs of trade union bureaucracies and their implications for trade union behaviour see Crouch, C., *Trade Unions: The Logic of Collective Action* (Fontana, Glasgow, 1982).
54. The extent to which this actually occurs clearly depends on whether work groups in particular establishments have the political capacity and skill to manipulate formal procedures in this way. For a pioneering attempt to identify the ideological and organisational characteristics of work groups in relation to their involvement in disputes procedures see Sayles, L., *Behaviour of Industrial Work Groups: Prediction and Control* (John Wiley, New York, 1958).

55. For the empirical examples of situations where this process had been taken to its extreme see Haraszti, M., *A Worker in a Worker's State* (Penguin, Harmondsworth, 1974); and Linhart, R., *The Assembly Line* (John Calder, London, 1981).
56. For an extended discussion of the concept of managerial prerogative and its ideological role in maintaining managerial control see Storey, J., *Managerial Prerogative and the Question of Control* (Routledge and Kegan Paul, London, 1983).
57. On this point see Armstrong, P., Goodman, J.F. and Hyman, J.P., *Ideology and Shop-Floor Industrial Relations* (Croom Helm, London, 1981).
58. For a number of empirical examples of this see Edwards, P.K., op. cit., (1986).
59. Friedman, H. and Meredeen, S., *The Dynamics of Industrial Conflict: Lessons from Ford* (Croom Helm, London, 1980).
60. Edwards, P.K. and Scullion, H., op. cit., (1982a).
61. Cressey, P., Eldridge, J.T. and MacInnes, J., *Just Managing: Authority and Democracy in Industry* (Open University Press, Milton Keynes, 1985).
62. Friedman, H. and Meredeen, S., op. cit., (1980), p. 35.
63. The illustration that Ford provides of a constitutionalist approach to the management of conflict is discussed in Purcell, J. and Sisson, K., op. cit., (1983).
64. The prime example of this exclusionary process, which provides the empirical focus for Friedman and Meredeen's study, is the women machinists' dispute of 1968 at Fords.
65. Edwards, P.K. and Scullion, H., op. cit., (1982a), pp. 238–44.
66. Cressey, P., Eldridge, J.T. and MacInnes, J., op. cit., (1985), p. 155.

5

MANAGEMENT AND CLASS

INTRODUCTION

The structural location and functional role of management within the class system of industrial capitalist societies remains an unresolved problem for contemporary class analysis.

Insofar as most forms of class analysis remain wedded to a dichotomous model of the class structures of advanced capitalist societies, the nature and significance of intermediate groupings or strata pose serious difficulties of a conceptual and substantive kind.[1] The latter have been exacerbated by the fact of the continued quantitative growth of the middle class and its increased socio-political significance for the character and direction of social change. Indeed, a number of commentators have suggested that the dynamics of structural change and socio-political reorganisation within the middle class will have a decisive impact upon the future pattern of power relationships emerging within advanced capitalist societies.[2]

The purpose of this chapter is to review the attempts that have been made to locate management within the analysis of contemporary class structure and their implications for the future development of the former as a strategic component of the stratification systems of advanced capitalistic societies.

With this end in view, four interrelated themes are pursued. First, a general review of Marxist and Weberian traditions of middle-class analysis, and of the more recent attempts to deal with the perceived

limitations of these approaches. Second, an exposition and assessment of the debate over the separation of ownership from control
and its implications for the class location and role of management.
Third, a review of two very different interpretive schemes that see
management either as part of the revolutionary vanguard of the new
working class or as the dominant sectional grouping within the
new middle class. Fourth, the central issue of the relationship
between class formation and collective action within what has come
to be called the service class will be discussed.

MANAGEMENT AND CLASS ANALYSIS

The manner in which management has been theorised within class
analysis is inseparable from the ways in which the 'embarrassment
of the middle classes'[3] has been handled by different analytical
perspectives as developed to deal with this problem.

Viewed from a Marxist perspective, the middle class (or classes)
poses two major problems, one conceptual and the other substantive. The conceptual problem concerns the theoretical difficulties
generated by the development of intermediate strata that undermine the logical consistency and analytical clarity of a dichotomous
model of the class structure 'proper' to advanced capitalist societies.
The substantive problem focuses upon the significance of a growing
middle-class stratum, which shows no sign of declining in size or
socio-political impact, for those forms of political intervention
which are most likely to realise a socialist society.

A Weberian perspective experiences rather different kinds of
problems. Its analytical sensitivity to the structural complexities
produced by the wide variations in market and work situations
experienced by different occupational groups makes it much more
responsive to the fragmentary character of contemporary stratification systems. However, this strength becomes a weakness when it
leads to a form of analysis in which the concept of class – as denoting
important social boundaries and potential bases for collective action – is dissolved into a multiplicity of competing interest groups
and deprived of any capacity to identify significant structural cleav-
ages within society.[4] Hindess summarises these difficulties in this
way:

The problem for Marxism is to identify the class positions of a large number of employees who are neither capitalists nor workers in the traditional sense . . . the result of attempts to conceptualize the positions of the new middle classes has been to weaken the clear cut division between those who possess means of production and those who do not. . . . The problems of Weberian analysis appear to be of a different order. Here it is a matter of how to avoid a fragmentation of the class structure given the enormous multiplicity of middle class occupations and market situations. The point is to bring order into that multiplicity by locating significant social boundaries within it.[5]

Much of the difficulty that both traditions experience with the analytical incorporation and empirical significance of the middle class stems from their very different theoretical starting points. From a Marxist perspective, class analysis must be rooted in the structure of social relations generated by the capitalist mode of production. It is the social relations connecting places within the division of labour created by the capitalist mode of production that provide the fundamental mechanisms controlling access to market opportunities relating to income, skill and task autonomy.[6] Weberian analysis, on the other hand, has tended to focus on the distributional aspects of class identified in terms of the quality of 'life-chances' made available to groups through their location within the labour market and place within the division of labour at work. In this way, class location and identity is defined in terms of the points of intersection between three factors:

Market situation, consisting of source and size of income, degree of job security, and opportunity for upward occupational mobility; work situation, or the set of social relationships in which the individual is involved at work by virtue of his position in the division of labour; and status situation, or the position in the hierarchy of prestige.[7]

The starting point of the Marxist perspective produces a two-class model that seems ill-equipped to cope with – descriptively, much less analytically – the obvious complexities of stratification systems that are not evolving in the direction of a more polarised and simplified structure of class relations. While being better equipped to deal with the increasing complexity and fragmentation evident in contemporary stratification systems, Weberian analysis seems to denude the concept of class of any explanatory purchase on structural change in advanced capitalist societies.

Growing dissatisfaction with the inadequacies of each of the above explanatory theories has produced attempts to develop them in such a way that they avoid the inherent limitations of earlier formulations. Within the Marxist perspective, the contributions of Carchedi,[8] Wright[9] and the Ehrenreichs[10] are important to the extent that they attempt to reformulate the focus of Marxist class analysis on production relations in such a way that it can incorporate the distributional complexities generated by the growth of the middle class. Within the Weberian perspective, the contributions of Giddens,[11] Parkin,[12] Goldthorpe[13] and Murphy[14] are significant in that they attempt to develop the Weberian focus on the interaction between market, work and status situation within the structure of power relations reproduced by capitalist economic systems.

Theoretical reformulation within the Marxist perspective takes the contradictory class location of various middle-class factions – such as managers – as its analytical starting point, but seems to terminate in a position not that dissimilar from that taken up by Weberian sociologists.[15] Managers are seen to occupy two places simultaneously within the class structure; they control the organisation of the capitalist production process, but they are also employees subjected to its economic imperatives. In this sense, their location indicates a form of class consciousness and action generally supportive of the institutional status quo prevailing under capitalist economic structures, but possessing the potential to question the political and ideological apparatus through which the latter are maintained. This potential resides in their knowledge of and exposure to the alienating effects of organisational control systems within capitalist enterprises.

However, this approach has increasingly been seen as theoretically unsatisfactory and empirically misleading. It remains wedded to a structuralist conception of class and is ill-equipped to deal with the complex socio-political processes whereby positional location in the class structure is translated into different forms of collective action. In response to these perceived inadequacies, recent formulations have focused upon organisational exploitation,[16] as providing a more acceptable analytical basis for drawing clear conceptual boundaries between the middle and working class, while at the same time serving to differentiate between various occupational groupings or fractions within the former. Thus, control over organisational assets such as authority structures and decision-making systems, access to scarce knowledge-based skills necessary to the reproduction of capitalist production relations, and the possession of institutionally recognised credentials such as degrees and diplomas provide the analytical foundations for reconstructing class relations within a Marxist perspective.

The reworking of class analysis within a Weberian approach has concerned itself with the range of social practices through which power has been mobilised to enhance or defend a group's position within the distributional order of rewards and resources. This has produced a focus upon the distributional conflicts taking place between and within classes under advanced capitalist regimes, and the role of these struggles in crystallising the overall patterns of class relations characteristic of the latter.[17] Yet, this overriding concern with the modes of collective action through which class relations emerge has been seen to obscure the wider structural context in which groups mobilise power to protect or improve their positions within the distributional order.[18]

These attempts at theoretical reformulation have produced a significant degree of convergence between the Marxist and Weberian perspectives in relation to the general question of the middle class and the more specific problem of the location and role of managers within the latter.[19] First, it entails a clear rejection of a wholly structural account of the middle class and raises fundamental issues concerning the processes whereby patterns of class interests and class relations are formed through collective struggle.[20] Second, it requires a refocusing of attention upon the different organisational forms through which dominant and subordinate groupings define their interests and mobilise power over time.[21] Third, it highlights the strategic significance of theoretical or technical knowledge for the analysis of higher level managerial and professional groupings within the middle class and its relationship to the distinctive modes of socio-economic organisation prevailing in contemporary capitalism.[22] Fourth, it suggests that a basic division within the middle class between lower-level white-collar workers performing routine tasks and higher-level functionaries may be crucial for an understanding of the class location and role of managers.[23]

However, each of these issues needs to be discussed against the backcloth provided by the debate over the separation of ownership from control and its implications for the development of a service class of professionals, technocrats and managers as discussed in the following section.

THE SEPARATION THESIS AND THE RISE OF THE SERVICE CLASS

The debate about the separation of ownership from control in modern industry focuses upon the most significant economic, political, organisational and technological changes that have occurred this century. As a number of commentators[24] have noted, it provides the intellectual backbone of a theory of socio-economic development that stands in stark contrast to that offered by Marxist social theory. Not only does it provide a coherent interpretation of the development and function of large-scale business corporations in contemporary social structures, but it also offers a systematic account of the major structural transformations occasioned by the evolution of industrial capitalism as the dominant societal type in the modern world. As such, it is the intellectual starting point for any understanding of modern systems of social stratifications that have emerged in the advanced capitalist societies.[25]

At the centre of this debate lies a series of interconnected propositions concerning the structural implications of certain economic changes consequent upon the growth of the large industrial joint-stock company. The work of Berle and Means[26] was the pioneering contribution in this debate because it offered a novel and persuasive explanation of the putative move to a radically different form of socio-economic system from that prevailing under classical or entrepreneurial capitalism during the nineteenth century.[27] Beed summarises the two major strands in Berle's writings in these terms:

> In most individual large companies, the control i.e. the individual or group who have the actual power to select the board of directors (or its majority) is not influenced by, subject to or identical with the ownership to any significant degree, for ownership is so widely distributed that no one individual or small group has even a minority interest large enough to

dominate the affairs of the company, so that management is left with substantially absolute power. The argument is then extended from the individual company to the corporate system as a whole to imply the direction of industry by persons other than those who have ventured their wealth. Generally, the system or collectivity is characterized by ownership of wealth without appreciable control and control of wealth without appreciable ownership.[28]

This suggests that the wide dispersal of share ownership resulting from the growth of the large-scale business corporation leads to a situation in which the power to control the composition of the board of directors and the direction of long-term corporate policy passes into the hands of a group of professional managers and technocrats who are effectively freed from the constraints of capitalist property ownership. Thus, strategic decision-making within the corporation concerned with the investment and allocation of large-scale capital funds became dominated by professional managers who would be primarily concerned with long-term economic stability and growth rather than short-term profit maximisation.[29] They had filled the power vacuum left by the decomposition of capital and the mass of dispersed, unorganised and apathetic shareholders left in its wake.

The theory of the managerial revolution, in its post-war versions, postulates that, with an increasing diffusion of stock ownership in many hands, effective control of corporate business is exercised by non-owning executives. Since the power of these managers derives from their positions in the bureaucratic hierarchies of business, not from wealth, their interests and motives differ from those of the older owner-entrepreneurs. Their control will be directed less to profit maximization as such than to other purposes, which may conflict with profit maximization: the maintenance and growth of the corporation as an end in itself; the interests of employees, customers, the public at large, as well as of shareholders.[30]

These economic changes were presumed to be linked to fundamental transformations in the organisation of political power, and the ideological legitimations through which they were rationalised, consequent upon the growth of the corporate state and the organisational society.[31] The bureaucratisation of private enterprises and public organisations, allied to their increasing reliance on the technical expertise provided by their managerial controllers,[32] was producing an independent class of higher level administrators, technocrats, professionals and managers that effectively controlled the corporate system. The institutional source of their power was located in their organisational expertise and its functional indispensability for the continuation of normal socio-economic life in a society dominated by an interlocking system of large-scale corporate enterprises. While proponents of the managerial revolution debated whether the power of this emergent class would be exercised in the furtherance of their own sectional interests or in the interest of some wider social constituency,[33] they were in total agreement that the powers of the propertied class had been appropriated by non-owning corporate managers. The latter now formed a new class of functionaries that dominated the strategic decision-making process setting the basic economic, social and technical parameters within which corporate enterprises would be operated.

Three central issues have structured the debate about the separation thesis and its implications for the changing class structures of advanced capitalist societies. Zeitlin summarises two of these issues in the following terms:

> Two issues have to be separated: (1) whether the large corporations continue to be controlled by ownership interests despite their management by functionaries who may themselves be propertyless; (2) whether the undisputed rise of the managerial functions means the rise of the functionaries themselves.[34]

The third issue focuses upon the social interests informing the social action of managers and their impact upon corporate behaviour. Useem summarises the three central tenets of the managerial revolution thesis in this way:

> The first is that the largest corporations are now more often than not controlled by managers not owners; the second is that managerial incentive systems are more closely tied to criteria other than company profitability; the third is that, as a result of the first and second changes, most large firms are now

oriented towards objectives beyond strict profit maximization.[35]

Critical evaluation of the three central tenets of the managerial
revolution thesis has concentrated upon its empirical foundations,
the theoretical extrapolations drawn from certain undisputed long-
term trends in the organisational forms characteristic of advanced
capitalist societies, and the substantive implications derived from
these extrapolations for changes to class structure and collective
action within the latter.[36]

As Child suggests,[37] a careful review of the empirical evidence
concerning changing patterns of ownership and control within
large-scale business corporations does not support the managerialist case. Rather, it indicates a restructuring – as opposed to a
complete break or divorce – of the relationship between patterns of
property ownership and the organisational mechanisms through
which corporate policy-making is controlled. More recently, Scott
has offered a detailed examination of the empirical evidence on
changing patterns of ownership and control in several advanced
capitalist societies, which indicates that:

> The prevailing form of ownership is now a de-personalized
> structure of intercorporate shareholdings, and the many fami-
> lies that survive as large shareholders become co-opted into a
> dominant group of finance capitalists with interests through-
> out the system. . . . In no case has control been divorced from
> ownership. Strategic control reflects the continuation of pro-
> prietary interests . . . The managerial revolution, far from
> nearing completion, has not yet begun.[38]

Some of the fiercest criticism of managerialist interpretations of
the rise of an autonomous and independent stratum of professional
managers and technocrats that exercises strategic control over the
corporation – freed from the structural and ideological constraints
imposed by capitalist property relations – has come from within a
Marxist perspective.[39] While accepting the case for a more extended and complex functional differentiation between ownership
interests and managerial interests, these critics firmly reject the
proposition that a process of institutional separation has occurred in
which the latter exercise autonomous control over the business
enterprise. Indeed, they maintain that changes to the institutional

forms through which modern capitalist economies are controlled have intensified, rather than reduced, the structural and ideological constraints that private ownership of the means of production imposes on managerial decision-making. As de Vroey puts it:

Marxists assert the lasting existing of the bourgeoise as a social class. It collectively holds shares of corporate ownership sufficiently concentrated to permit it to monopolize the power of assignment and disposition of the means of production and to use this power for its specific class interests, i.e. to produce and realize surplus value.[40]

This position clearly implies that company profitability and the continuous search for more effective means of increasing capital accumulation remain the overriding structural imperatives within which managers are forced to operate. Senior managers and directors identify very closely with the long-term aims and priorities of dominant shareholding interests in which sustained profit maximisation remains the major concern.[41] The crucial significance assigned to the long-term economic interests of private owners and their institutional representatives in banks, pension funds and insurance companies is reinforced by kinship ties and modes of cultural socialisation supportive of capitalist values and aspirations.[42] As Hamilton and Hirszowicz conclude:

The motives, goals, values and attitudes of those senior executives who come from this kind of background are not likely, then, to differ from those of the traditional capitalist employer. Furthermore, now, there is little reason to suppose that the motives and behaviour of managers who do not come from such a background differ very much either. There is little reason to suppose that professional salaried managers who do have some degree of autonomy and control over their firms behave any differently from traditional owners and controllers. The idea that professional salaried management is less profit oriented is not very plausible.[43]

However, none of these criticisms – taken in isolation or as a complete package – has been of sufficient force to deny the sustained growth of a service class of higher level managers, professionals and technocrats who have a distinctive class location and role when compared to the upper class of corporate owners and controllers on the one hand, and the working class of manual labourers on the other.[44] Nor have they undermined belief in the continued significance of this service class for an understanding of the internal power struggles to control strategic decision-making within business firms and their impact on the wider network of inter-corporate relations in which they are embedded. As Scott[45] indicates, this service class is a significant component of the dominant coalition of entrepreneurs, financiers, bankers and internal managers, who seek to impose their, often conflicting, interests and priorities on corporate strategy. Their technical knowledge, information processing capacities and organisational skills have become crucial to the long-term profitability that secures survival and prosperity in a highly competitive market.[46] This can provide an effective power base from which to exert considerable influence within the external networks of inter-corporate networks in which their individual firms operate.

Indeed, a spate of more recent publications[47] has suggested that the service class must assume a crucial explanatory role in accounting for large-scale structural transformations occurring in contemporary capitalism and their longer term implications for future institutional development. Goldthorpe supports the argument for treating professional, administrative and managerial employees as holding similar class positions in the following terms:

> These employees, in being typically engaged in the exercise of delegated authority or in the application of specialist knowledge and expertise, operate in their work tasks and roles with a distinctive degree of autonomy and discretion; and in direct consequence of the element of trust that is thus necessarily involved in their relationship with their employing organization, they are accorded conditions of employment which are also distinctive in both the level and kinds of rewards involved. In other words, professional, administrative and managerial employees are in these ways typically differentiated from other grades of employee – and most obviously from wage earners – in the character of both their work and market situations. Given this conception of the basis of a service class, it then becomes possible in turn to treat fairly systematically various issues which arise concerning both its internal divisions and its 'boundaries' with other classes.[48]

However, as Goldthorpe notes, the interests that are linked to these service class positions in private and public sector corporate bureaucracies, and the pattern of socio-political action flowing from them, are very difficult to discern. Two, very different, interpretations have been offered: first, that which treats higher and middle level managerial and technical personnel as the radical vanguard of a new working class challenging the dominance of the upper class owners and controllers; second, that which views them as the key component within a new middle class with distinctive class interests in opposition to those of both traditional dominant and subordinate class groupings in contemporary capitalism. Each of these interpretations will be reviewed before proceeding to the elucidation of more general conclusions concerning the relationship between class formation and action within the service class and its implications for longer-term social change.

THE NEW WORKING CLASS

The proposition that technological and organisational changes in the most advanced sectors of industrial capitalist societies were producing a new category of middle stratum occupations, opposed to the dominant socio-economic interests of the owning class, was originally adumbrated by French social theorists such as Mallet[49] and Touraine.[50] Mallet expresses this thesis in the following terms:

In fact, the more important research, invention and quality control become, the more human work becomes concentrated in the preparation and organization of production, the more the sense of initiative and responsibility increase; to put it briefly, the more the modern worker reconquers on the collective level the professional autonomy which he had lost during the period of the mechanization of work, the more will demands for control develop. Today's conditions of production offer objective possibilities for the development of generalized self-management of production and the economy by those who carry the weight. But these possibilities are confronted simultaneously by the capitalist structures of the relations of production, its criteria of profitability based on the short-term profit of the owners, and the technocratic structure of the firms which seem more to inhibit the harmonious development of their own productive possibilities. The recent social conflicts, which have developed during the last few years in the West, and the strike of May 1968 which crowned this series of movements, have shown that the advanced sectors of the working class are no longer content to make wage demands. Indeed, they challenged the techno-bureaucratic centres which direct the economy, to such an extent that they no longer seemed to be justified by developing technical and economic needs.[51]

In this sense, the new working class performs a dual function within the emerging class structures and related forms of socio-political action characteristic of advanced capitalist societies; they challenge the economic imperatives of exploitation and accumulation underlying capitalist property relations and they radicalise the rest of the old working class of manual labourers in social struggles fostering an ideological awareness that goes beyond the wage bargain. This professionally educated and highly trained cadre of middle level managerial, scientific and technical employees will provide the vanguard of the traditional working class. They are mounting the only serious challenge to the capitalist imperatives of accumulation and profitability informing contemporary structures of organisational control. At the same time, they possess the ideological and political skills necessary to bring the traditional working class with them by expanding their consciousness beyond the narrow confines of collective bargaining. Thus, it is the specialist knowledge and expertise of the new working class that provides them with the intellectual power base from which they can challenge capitalist domination within a production system where access to and control over information is becoming the key resource.[52] In addition, their organisational location at strategic points within the control systems of technologically advanced industries – such as chemicals, gas, oil, electronics, computers and engineering – provides the institutional framework through which their skills can be deployed in the furtherance of industrial and political action aimed at transforming authoritarian structures in the direction of self-management and workers' control.

The debate that has ensued over the empirical foundations and theoretical cogency of the new working class thesis has usually taken a highly critical form.[53] The latter has focused upon a number of deficiencies within the thesis concerning its predilection for technological determinism; its tendency to underestimate the continuing significance of hierarchical control structures in advanced industries; its supposition that knowledge has supplanted technology as the primary productive force in contemporary capitalist systems; its rather ill-defined and ambiguous analytical identification of the new working class as constituting a social class; and its assumption that members of the latter will possess and project a revolutionary consciousness that is opposed to that of the dominant owning class and can overcome the innate economism of the traditional working class (that is, its almost exclusive concern with the wage packet).

The cumulative impact of these criticisms has been to inflict such severe damage on the new working class thesis that an alternative interpretation has been formulated which focuses upon internal differentiation within the middle class and its implications for contemporary socio-political practice.

THE NEW MIDDLE CLASS

The continued expansion of white collar occupational groupings and its impact on the stratification systems of capitalist societies in the direction of a more complex and highly differentiated – not to say fragmented – class structure has been a major topic of sociological analysis and political debate since the earlier decades of this century.[54] However, this debate has been considerably extended and intensified in more recent years as developments in economic organisation and the division of labour[55] have contributed to the explosive growth of a wide range of managerial, administrative, technical and professional jobs constituting a new middle class distinct from that of the old middle class of traders, shopkeepers, self-employed entrepreneurs and the liberal professions.

The distinctiveness of the former groups is presumed to reside, not only in their shared occupational situations and organisational locations, but also in their characteristic type of class imagery. The old middle class are seen to be generally conservative, not to say right-wing, in their ideological views and express strong fears of being caught in a pincer movement between a large and aggressive working class on the one hand, and an economically and politically powerful owning class on the other. The new middle class articulate a much more complex, not to say contradictory, form of class imagery where a defensive and self-interested attitude towards their present levels of economic reward, delegated authority and social status is combined with a progressive view of the need to maintain and protect state support for the social wage in circumstances where it may be under threat.[56]

Contemporary discussion about the new middle class has been concentrated upon the emergence of a much more explicit and rigid division within the ranks of the middle class between the mass of lower level white collar workers performing routine tasks in large bureaucracies and a numerically smaller group of higher level functionaries who are more appropriately included within the service class. Both in terms of market situation and work situation, the former group are seen to be subject to a process of proletarianisation where their levels of remuneration and degree of job autonomy have been subjected to long-term deterioration and deskilling similar to that experienced by manual workers. In turn, this has had a negative effect on their social status whereby they are increasingly seen as more appropriately relocated within the ranks of the labouring classes.[57] Service class personnel, in direct contrast, are seen to have enjoyed considerable improvements in their market, work and status situations such that they now occupy a strategic position within the stratification system of advanced capitalist societies and perform technical and organisational roles crucial to their survival. Abercrombie and Urry summarise this polarisation between a white-collar proletariat and a managerial service class in the following manner:

> We conclude that it is fair to refer to the market and work situation of deskilled white collar workers as proletarianized; the class places of these workers are subject to forces similar to those of the working class. . . . In considering the market situation of the service class at various points our conclusion is that there is a substantial divergence of pay and various fringe benefits between the service class and deskilled white collar workers. Another important point of difference in the market situation of these two groups lies in the notion of career . . . service class places also involve a relative freedom from control, providing a sphere of autonomy within which it is

possible to organize and pace work as one likes, taking responsibility for the work done . . . the service class performs the functions of control, reproduction and conceptualization – necessary functions in relationship to labour.[58]

The theme of the functional role of the service class within the capitalist mode of production and its implications for the form of socio-political action in which the former is likely to engage has provided a focal point for more recent analysis.

As Dahrendorf[59] notes, one of the most significant characteristics of the service class is its location within and dependence upon bureaucratic organisations. Both the economic position and political power of the service class are closely linked to the expansion of bureaucratic structures – particularly in the tertiary section of employment – and the opportunities they provide for career rewards involving steady improvements in pay, conditions and job autonomy. The most important feature of the bureaucratic roles performed by members of the service class is described by Dahrendorf in this way:

The main expectation attached to service class positions is the administration of laws, whether public or private, formal or sanctioned. This involves their adaptation to individual cases, their reformulation, their publication, their enforcement. The service class provides a bridge between rulers and ruled. But the direction of the road does not and must not change on this bridge. More than any other social category, the service class is committed to the ruling norms which it administers without having made them; more than others, the members of this class tend to be 'conformist'.[60]

In this way, Dahrendorf concludes that the service class will have a 'conservative' political orientation, given its status as an appendage to the ruling groups within society and its fealty to the latter as a defence against any encroachments on its power and influence. Consequently, the service class is defined in terms of the functions that are delegated to it by the capitalist class and the material and ideological commitments they are presumed to instill in support of the institutional status quo. Abercrombie and Urry argue that the service class 'performs the functions of control, reproduction and conceptualization – necessary functions for capital in relationship to labour'.[61] Members of the service class design labour processes in which there is a clear separation between mental and manual labour, where the commodities produced within those processes can be separated from the direct producers, and where continuous surveillance and control can be exercised over the latter. These authors maintain that the capacity of the service class to shape and reshape social structures is relatively strong in contemporary capitalism and suggest that its 'causal powers' will be directed towards the restructuring of:

> capitalist societies so as to maximize the divorce between conception and execution and to ensure the elaboration of highly differentiated and specific structures within which knowledge and science can be maximally developed. They are thus to deskill productive labourers and to maximize the educational requirements of places within the social division of labour. This implies the minimizing of non-educational/ non-achievement criteria for recruitment to such places; and the maximizing of income resources devoted to education and science, and more generally to the sphere of 'reproduction'. The middle classes will thus possess powers to enlarge the state structures by which they can organize and 'service' capitalist enterprises.[62]

Clearly, Abercrombie and Urry are much more sensitive to the revolutionary potential of the service class insofar as their analysis points to its willingness and capacity to restructure organisational and technical relationships in order to enhance its economic position and political power. However, the extent to which its causal powers will be exercised to defend or transform the dominant institutional structures prevailing in advanced capitalist societies is the subject of considerable controversy.

Some commentators[63] have suggested that a professional managerial class has emerged within monopoly capitalism with an ideological *Weltanschauung* that inevitably brings it into conflict with the capitalist class. Committed to the values of efficiency, order and rationality, members of the professional managerial class find themselves demanding a degree of occupational autonomy and control that is at odds with their continued subordination to the owning class and its demand for profit maximisation. Professional ideologies extolling the value of disinterested service and community care combine with occupational self-interests in autonomy and control to form within the middle class a vanguard group that possesses the potential to challenge capitalist imperatives and the structures of domination they require. The strategic location of this group in performing critical knowledge-based functions of scientific/technical innovation and managerial control within the political economy of contemporary capitalism provides a power-base from which this challenge may be mounted.

Other commentators[64] have seriously questioned this interpretation of the political orientation and strategy of the service class. Goldthorpe encapsulates this alternative interpretation when he argues that the evident expansion and consolidation of the service class within contemporary capitalism does not mean that its members will necessarily formulate and implement a socio-political strategy that presents any fundamental threat to the prevailing social order. Indeed, he gives general support to Dahrendorf's contention that the service class constitutes an essentially 'conservative' element within modern societies, given its substantial stake in the status quo and its willingness to use superior resources – of a material, political and cultural kind – to preserve its position of relative power and social advantage. While there is a strengthening tendency for service class groupings to pursue their socio-economic interests through various forms of collective action and organisation – including trade union organisation[65] – this is most appropriately interpreted as 'an attempt to prevent proletarianization and to maintain favourable class differentials in pay and conditions and in life chances generally'.[66]

Nevertheless, Goldthorpe does identify one source of dissatisfaction that may generate disaffection within the ranks of the service class – that is, the threats to their security and prospects entailed in neo-liberal policies aimed at drastically reducing the public sector in favour of reviving and reinforcing capitalist incentives and discipline. However, Goldthorpe suggests that this is likely to produce socio-political orientations and strategies within the service class supportive of corporatist values and institutions in which the ideology and practice of meritocracy can be more safely protected and advanced in opposition to neo-liberal deregulation or socialist egalitarianism.

Both of these interpretations have recently been challenged in a fundamental way by the analysis presented by Lash and Urry.[67] These authors contend that the 'causal powers' of the service class were considerably enhanced after World War II and that these powers have been used in such a way that both the socio-political developmental trajectories and economic structures of contemporary capitalist societies have been completely transformed. They also suggest that this transformation has produced a situation in which the interests of the service class are not necessarily coincidental with that of the capitalist class, insofar as certain groupings[68] within the former are committed to values and institutions resistant to the unrestrained imposition of the imperatives of exploitation and accumulation. Indeed, the service class is the primary social change agent whereby organised capitalism has been transformed into disorganised capitalism – that is, a systematic process of disaggregation and restructuration that has broken down and fragmented the highly concentrated and centralised social structures typical of organised capitalism.[69]

Lash and Urry characterise the position and function of the service class in terms of non-ownership places within the social division of labour which service capital accumulation and enjoy advantageous work and market situations regulated by the differential possession of credentials attesting to its members' superior knowledge and expertise. They further maintain that the rise of the service class was due not to the logic of capitalist accumulation or the demands of modern technology, but rather to the growth of scientific, rational management, which entailed a substantial break with the trajectory of capitalist development.[70] This was true to the extent that the expansion and increasing power of the service class – at the expense of both capitalist and working classes – generated a series of interconnected socio-political processes that fragmented and disorganised centralised structures within the political economies of capitalist societies after World War II. The development of an educationally based stratification system, the growth of new social movements and the sectionalisation of class politics have their source in the continued growth of a knowledge-based service class 'which serves capital but increasingly does so on its own terms'.[71]

Whatever differences of analysis and interpretation exist between these alternative perspectives on the significance of the new middle class for an understanding of class structures and strategies within contemporary capitalism, they all point to the fact that the socio-political orientations and actions 'of the new middle stratum which these positions comprise has critical implications for both representative politics and for class struggle'.[72] This latter theme requires further elucidation.

CLASS FORMATION AND COLLECTIVE ACTION

Goldthorpe argues that the link between class position and class action is highly problematical to the extent that it is forged by processes of class formation concerned with:

> the extent to which classes acquire a demographic identity – that is, become identifiable as collectivities through the continuity with which individuals and families retain their class positions over time; and second those associated with the extent to which classes acquire a socio-cultural identity – that is, become identifiable through the shared and distinctive life-styles of their members and their patterns of preferred association.[73]

Thus, the degree to which a class exhibits a clear demographic identity and a coherent cultural identity is clearly dependent upon economic, technological, organisational and ideological conditions, which can vary considerably over time and place. The degree of formation exhibited by the service class is a particular problem for a number of reasons connected with the ambiguities of the structure of power relationships in which middle stratum positions develop:

> professionals and managers are largely dependent and reliant upon institutions of capital for any vestiges of control which may be retained by their occupations. We would suggest that this creates insurmountable problems for any theoretical determination concerning their class formation.[74]

This view is supported by Goldthorpe's analysis, which indicates that the wide recruitment base and highly variable levels of education and training evident within the service class leads to a low degree of demographic and cultural identity. This seems to indicate that while the capacity of the service class to reproduce and expand itself is undiminished, its ability to engage in collective action – with or without other class groupings – is severely limited.

Nevertheless, this does not mean that collective action on the part of service class groupings is impossible; neither does it entail the proposition that such action which does occur will have a negligible impact on existing institutional structures. The service class may be internally divided between a public-sector-based grouping commit- ted to a corporatist strategy and a private-sector-based grouping adhering to a neo-liberal strategy of socio-economic development. Yet, both the direction and content of class politics are likely to be substantially influenced by the organisational forms through which sectors of the service class – possibly in temporary alliance with other class groupings or movements – struggle to preserve and enhance their interests in opposition to other classes.

As Hindess argues, classes do not directly engage in political action; it is organisations such as political parties, trade unions, employers' associations and state agencies that are involved in political struggle. The connections between class interests and organisational action are extremely difficult to establish and depend upon 'definite discursive and other kinds of conditions, and their identification is always open to dispute. Interests are not fixed or given properties of individuals or groups, and they should not be regarded as structurally determined'.[75] This leads Hindess to sug- gest that the central question in the analysis of political action is the issue of the organisational forms in and through which groups of social actors formulate and pursue their shared interests as these have emerged out of their 'assessment of the conditions they confront and in locating themselves and others in relation to these conditions and possible changes in them'.[76]

Thus, the organisational practices in and through which sectors of the service class attempt to pursue their discursively formulated interests remain a crucial issue for any analysis of political struggle and its institutional implications in contemporary capitalist societies. These organisational practices and the structures they reproduce are the principal mechanisms through which different class groupings engage in political action and assess its conse- quences for realising their interests and values.

CONCLUSION

This chapter has reviewed the way in which management has been treated within the analysis of contemporary class structures and strategies. It has clearly indicated that the argument about the rise of a service class of professional, administrative and managerial employees that will have a fundamental impact upon the direction and content of future socio-political development has much to commend itself to sociologists dealing with the analysis of institutional change.

The opportunities and threats posed by contemporary socio-economic conditions to the members of this service class and the manner in which they are likely to respond will be discussed in the next chapter.

REFERENCES

1. For an elaboration of this point see Abercrombie, N. and Urry, J., *Capital, Labour and the Middle Classes* (Allen and Unwin, London, 1983); Carter, B., *Capitalism, Class Conflict and the New Middle Class* (Routledge and Kegan Paul, London, 1985); Hindess, B., *Politics and Class Analysis* (Basil Blackwell, Oxford, 1987).
2. Goldthorpe, J.H., 'On the Service Class: Its Formation and Future', in Giddens, A. and Mackenzie, G. (eds.), *Social Class and Division of Labour* (Cambridge University Press, Cambridge, 1982), pp. 162–85; Clegg, S., Boreham, P. and Dow, G., *Class, Politics and the Economy* (Routledge and Kegan Paul, London, 1986); Lash, S. and Urry, J., *The End of Organized Capitalism* (Polity Press, Oxford, 1987).
3. Hindess, op. cit., (1987), p. 53. For some analysts, this is less of an embarrassment and more of a celebration of the highly differentiated and diversified stratification systems discovered in contemporary capitalism. On this point see Roberts, K., Cook, F.G., Clark, S.C. and Semeonoft, E., *The Fragmentary Class Structure* (Heinemann, London, 1977).
4. See Abercrombie and Urry, op. cit., (1983) and Hindess, op. cit., (1987), for more extended treatment of these points.
5. Hindess, op. cit., (1987), pp. 71–2.
6. For a more detailed exposition of the contrast between Marxist and Weberian conceptualisations of class, which emphasises the presumed analytical and explanatory limitations of the latter, see Crompton, R. and Gubbay, J., *Economy and Class Structure* (Macmillan, London, 1977).
7. Abercrombie and Urry, op. cit., (1983), p. 20.
8. Carchedi, G., *On the Economic Identification of Social Classes* (Routledge and Kegan Paul, London, 1977).
9. Wright, E.O., *Classes* (Verso, London, 1985).
10. Ehrenreich, B. and Ehrenreich, J., 'The Professional-Managerial Class', in Walker, P. (ed.), *Between Labour and Capital* (South End Press, Boston, 1979), pp. 5–45. For a more selective analysis of the

location and role of professional occupations and groups within the class structure see Johnson, T., 'The Professions in the Class Structure', in Scase, R. (ed.), *Industrial Society: Class, Cleavage and Control* (Allen and Unwin, London, 1977), pp. 93–110.

11. Giddens, A., *The Class Structure of the Advanced Societies* (Hutchinson, London, 2nd edition, 1981).

12. Parkin, F., *Marxism and Class Theory: A Bourgeois Critique* (Tavistock, London, 1979).

13. Goldthorpe, J.H., *Social Mobility and the Class Structure in Modern Britain* (Clarendon Press, Oxford, 1980).

14. Murphy, R., 'The Structure of Closure: A Critique and Development of the Theories of Weber, Collins and Parkin', *British Journal of Sociology*, vol. 35, (1984), pp. 547–67 and 'The Concept of Class in Closure Theory', *Sociology*, vol. 20, (1986), pp. 247–64.

15. For a review of these developments, which takes a rather more critical line on the putative convergence between Marx and Weber on class theory, see Nichols, T., 'Introduction', in Armstrong, P., Carter, B., Smith, C. and Nichols, T., *White Collar Workers, Trade Unions and Class* (Croom Helm, London, 1986), pp. 1–18.

16. For a review and critique of Wright's recent contribution to this debate see Rose, D. and Marshall, G., 'Constructing The (W)Right Classes', *Sociology*, vol. 20, (1986), pp. 440–55.

17. See Rose and Marshall, op. cit., (1986).

18. See Murphy, op. cit., (1986).

19. For a dissenting voice and an attempt to reassert the analytical clarity and explanatory adequacy of the two-class model see Barbalet, J.M., 'Limitations of Class Theory and the Disappearance of Status: The Problem of the New Middle Class', *Sociology*, vol. 20, (1986), pp. 557–76.

20. This point is made with substantial force in Rose and Marshall, op. cit., (1986).

21. On this point see Lash, S. and Urry, J. 'The New Marxism of Collective Action: A Critical Analysis', *Sociology*, vol. 18, (1984), pp. 33–50.

22. See Abercrombie and Urry, op. cit., (1983).

23. Ibid., pp. 110–27.

24. Child, J., *The Business Enterprise in Modern Industrial Society* (Collier-Macmillan, London, 1969); Nichols, T., *Ownership, Control and Ideology* (Allen and Unwin, London, 1969); Scott, J., *Corporations, Classes and Capitalism* (Hutchinson, London, 2nd edition, 1985).

25. Westergaard, J.H., 'The Withering Away of Class: A Contemporary Myth', in Anderson, P. and Blackburn, R. (eds.), *Towards Socialism* (Fontana, London, 1965), pp. 77–113.

26. Berle, A.A. and Means, G.C., *The Modern Corporation and Private Property* (Macmillan, New York, 1932).

27. Berle, A.A., *Power Without Property* (Harcourt Brace, New York, 1960).

28. Beed, C.S., 'The Separation of Ownership from Control', in Gilbert, M. (ed.), *The Modern Business Enterprise* (Penguin, Harmondsworth, 1982), pp. 137–52 (p. 137).
29. Marris, R., *The Economic Theory of 'Managerial' Capitalism* (Macmillan, London, 1964). Also see the contributions to Marris, R. (ed.), *The Corporate Society* (Macmillan, London, 1974).
30. Westergaard, op. cit., (1965), p. 96.
31. Burnham, J., *The Managerial Revolution* (Penguin, Harmondsworth, 1945); Crosland, A., *The Future of Socialism* (Jonathan Cape, London, 1956); Dahrendorf, R., *Class and Class Conflict in Industrial Society* (Routledge and Kegan Paul, London, 1959); Presthus, R.V., *The Organizational Society* (Macmillan, London, 2nd edition, 1978).
32. On the centrality of the concept of the technostructure of middle-level administrators, managers and scientists for an understanding of the distribution of power within the modern corporate system see Galbraith, J.K., *The New Industrial State* (Penguin, Harmondsworth, 1969).
33. This question is addressed at some length in Nichols, T., op. cit., (1969), and Fidler, J., *The British Business Elite: Its Attitudes to Class, Status and Power* (Routledge and Kegan Paul, London, 1981). Sectional managerialism maintains that managers will act rationally to pursue their own economic and political interests; non-sectional managerialism envisages the growth of a purely neutral technocracy that will follow socially responsible policies balancing the competing claims of various corporate stakeholders such as shareholders, workers, consumers and voters.
34. Zeitlin, M., 'Corporate Ownership and Control: The Large Corporation and the Capitalist Class', *American Journal of Sociology*, vol. 79, (1973–4), pp. 1073–1119 (p. 1078).
35. Useem, M., *The Inner Circle: Large Corporations and the Rise of Business Political Activity in the US and UK* (Oxford University Press, Oxford, 1984), p. 29.
36. For two recently published overviews of the managerial thesis see Clegg, Boreham and Dow, op. cit., (1986), and Hamilton, M. and Hirszowicz, M., *Class and Inequality in the Pre-Industrial, Capitalist and Communist Societies* (Wheatsheaf Books, Sussex, 1987).
37. Child, op. cit., (1969).
38. Scott, op. cit., (1985), pp. 259–60.
39. For example see Miliband, R., *The State in Capitalist Society* (Weidenfeld and Nicholson, London, 1967); Blackburn, R., 'The New Capitalism', in Blackburn, R. (ed.), *Ideology in Social Science: Readings in Critical Social Theory* (Fontana, London, 1972), pp. 164–86; Sweezy, P.M., *Modern Capitalism and Other Essays* (Monthly Review Press, New York, 1972); Zeitlin, op. cit., (1974); Westergaard, J. and Resler, H., *Class in a Capitalist Society: A Study of Contemporary Britain* (Penguin, Harmondsworth, 1976); Salaman, G., *Class and the Corporation* (Fontana, London, 1981). For a highly critical assessment of the Marxist perspective on managerialism, which adopts a conception

of the business firm very close to that advocated in this book, see Johnston, L., *Marxism, Class Analysis and Socialist Pluralism* (Allen and Unwin, London, 1986).

40. de Vroey, Michel, 'A Marxist View of Ownership and Control', in Nichols, T. (ed.), *Capital and Labour: A Marxist Primer* (Fontana, London, 1980), pp. 218–36 (p. 226).

41. For empirical evidence supporting this conclusion see Nichols, op. cit., (1969); Fidler, op. cit., (1981); Poole, M., Mansfield, R., Blyton, P. and Frost, P., *Managers in Focus: The British Manager in the Early 1980s* (Gower, Aldershot, 1981).

42. For empirical evidence on this point see Urry, J. and Wakeford, J. (eds.), *Power in Britain* (Heinemann, London, 1973); Stanworth, P. and Giddens, A. (eds.), *Elites and Power in British Society* (Cambridge University Press, Cambridge, 1974).

43. Hamilton and Hirszowicz, op. cit., (1987), p. 121.

44. Abercrombie and Urry, op. cit., (1983).

45. Scott, op. cit., (1985).

46. For an empirical case study that illustrates this point and highlights the need to forge a closer theoretical relationship between labour process analysis and circuits of capital see Morgan, G. and Hooper, D., 'Corporate Strategy, Ownership and Control', *Sociology*, vol. 21, (1987), pp. 609–27.

47. Urry, J., *Scientific Management and the Service Class* (Lancaster Regionalism Group, University of Lancaster, Working Paper 12, 1984); Clegg, Boreham and Dow, op. cit., (1986); Hamilton and Hirszowicz, op. cit., (1987); and Lash and Urry, op. cit., (1987).

48. Goldthorpe, op. cit., (1982), p. 169. The analytical roots of Goldthorpe's characterisation in Weberian class theory are closely expressed in this quotation.

49. Mallet, S., *The New Working Class* (Spokesmen Books, Nottingham, 1975).

50. Touraine, A., *The Post-Industrial Society* (Wildwood House, London, 1974).

51. Mallet, op. cit., (1975), pp. 28–9.

52. Smith, C., *Technical Workers: Class, Labour and Trade Unionism* (Macmillan, London, 1987), pp. 21–3.

53. On this point see Mann, M., *Consciousness and Action Among the Western Working Class* (Macmillan, London, 1973); Gallie, D., *In Search of the New Working Class* (Cambridge University Press, Cambridge, 1978); Low-Beer, J.R., *Protest and Participation: The New Working Class in Italy* (Cambridge University Press, Cambridge, 1978); Giddens, A., op. cit., (1981); Hyman, R., 'White-Collar Workers and Theories of Class', in Hyman, R. and Price, R. (eds.), *The New Working Class? White-Collar Workers and their Organizations* (Macmillan, London, 1983), pp. 3–45; Clegg, Boreham and Dow, op. cit., (1986); Smith, op. cit., (1987).

54. This point is developed in greater detail in Carter, op. cit., (1985).

55. Empirical material relating to British trends in these areas is reviewed

in some detail in Hyman, op. cit., (1983).
56. Roberts, *et al.*, op. cit., (1977).
57. Hamilton and Hirszowicz, op. cit., (1987).
58. Abercrombie and Urry, op. cit., (1983), pp. 118–22.
59. Dahrendorf, R., 'The Service Class', in Burns, T. (ed.), *Industrial Man* (Penguin, Harmondsworth, 1969), pp. 140–50.
60. Ibid., p. 145.
61. Abercrombie and Urry, op. cit., (1983), p. 122.
62. Ibid., p. 132.
63. Ehrenreich and Ehrenreich, op. cit., (1979).
64. Goldthorpe, op. cit., (1982); Hyman, op. cit., (1983); Clegg, Boreham and Dow, op. cit., (1986); Hamilton and Hirszowicz, op. cit., (1987).
65. This issue is discussed at greater length in the next chapter.
66. Goldthorpe, op. cit., (1982), p. 181.
67. Lash and Urry, op. cit., (1987).
68. Here, Lash and Urry contrast the interests and action of the public sector and private sector wings of the service class.
69. Lash and Urry maintain that the increased power and influence of the service class is functional for the process of capital accumulation. However, they suggest that the service class is likely to oppose, and become more independent of, the capitalist class as class struggle in disorganised capitalism bcomes even more fragmented and sectionalised.
70. For an elaboration of this point comparing developments in America and Britain during the early decades of this century see Urry, op. cit., (1984).
71. Lash and Urry, op. cit., (1987), p. 194.
72. Clegg, Boreham and Dow, op. cit., (1986), p. 169.
73. Goldthorpe, op. cit., (1982), pp. 171–2.
74. Clegg, Boreham and Dow, op. cit., (1986), p. 165.
75. Hindess, op. cit., (1987), pp. 112–13. As Johnston expresses the point: ' . . . political interests and objectives can never be separated from their organizational context'. Johnston, op. cit., (1986), p. 129.
76. Hindess, op. cit., (1987), p. 120.

6

MANAGERIAL FUTURES

INTRODUCTION

The preceding chapters of this book have focused upon management as a complex, not to say contradictory, social practice geared to the assembly and control of other practices concerned with productive activity. They have also attempted to provide some insight into the characteristic tensions and predicaments faced by its practitioners in their role as organisational functionaries and as members of larger social class groupings engaged in conflict with other collective agents.

The purpose of this chapter is to identify the challenges posed to management by large-scale structural changes taking place in the political economy and the responses that are available to them in dealing with the opportunities and threats the former present. Three interrelated structural transformations and their long-term implications are highlighted: technological, organisational and occupational change. Three potential responses to the socio-economic transformations wrought by developments in these areas are discussed: professionalisation, unionisation and privatisation. A concluding section will examine the possibility that we are currently witnessing the beginning of the end of management as we have come to know it in advanced capitalist societies.

TECHNOLOGICAL CHANGE

The long-term impact of technological change on both the quantity and quality of employment made available to managers has recently emerged as a significant issue in contemporary sociological research and analysis. A great deal of attention has previously been directed towards the severe reductions in workers' capacities to preserve jobs, maintain work skills and retain control over the pacing and intensity of productive processes brought about by the introduction of new technologies.[1] While management has usually been seen as the agent of this deskilling process, more recent research and debate have begun to shift towards a concern with the role of managers as victims of technological change.[2] Indeed, these studies are beginning to suggest that the substantial reductions in autonomy, skill and control in the work situations of shop-floor workers produced by the introduction of microelectronic technologies are now being experienced within the ranks of lower and middle management.[3] The extent to which groups of higher-level and specialist managers located within the ranks of the service class are in a position to resist pressures towards work degradation is a moot point.[4]

The long-term effects of new technology on the number of jobs available in first-line and middle management has recently been assessed by Gill. He indicates that the introduction of microelectronic technology in the office and on the factory floor is likely to produce substantial reductions in a wide range of supervisory and managerial jobs as automated administration with linked decentralised control systems replaces more direct and personalised forms of control:

> the office sector is ripe for technological innovation . . . all the indications are that there will be less demand for office services in the future because the increasing automation in manufacturing will not require human co-ordination in offices between different steps in the production process that are currently involved . . . there will be a trend towards more concentration in the provision of office services, as small firms find it more convenient to contract-out some of their activities to larger centres of information-processing.[5]

This assessment is supported by Child's view that all the evidence on the introduction of microelectronic technology points to a re-centralisation of control in most work organisations in Britain. This is consistent with an employment policy 'which aims at consolidating a small élite of senior managers and associated specialist and technical personnel within a primary sector of the labour market while placing other employees into a secondary segment and/or into the external labour market'.[6] He also sees the content of managerial work and the structure of management organisation being substantially changed by modern information technology. There is likely to be a reduction in the numbers of managerial staff in the lower and middle ranges of the organisational hierarchy, while those jobs that remain in these sectors will be almost wholly concerned with routine information-processing and monitoring functions. These economies in lower and middle-level managerial manpower are likely to be combined with a simplification and compression of management hierarchies such that senior managers will be able to exert more effective centralised and depersonalised control over organisational operations. Microelectronic technology will provide the hardware through which top-level management can unify and co-ordinate previously fragmented control systems in such a way that the *raison d'être* for lower and middle-level management's continued existence is all but removed.

However, members of the service class are unlikely to escape totally unscathed from the chilling embrace of microelectronic technology. Child's research on the introduction of information technology, combining microprocessing with electronic communications, in the work situations of administrators, managers and professionals, reveals the extension of 'rationalization upwards within white collar hierarchies'.[7] His review of the impact of new technology upon service-class occupations in both the public-service sector and the private and commercial sectors points to a general trend eroding the privileged employment position of higher-level white-collar workers. This is true to the extent that their work situations are now subjected to pressures for simplification and standardisation in task performance previously reserved for blue-collar workers, and their labour market situation is increasingly dependent upon the policies of their employing organisations. The loss of autonomy, associated with technologically induced rationalisation, and the increasing economic dependence, associated with organisational subordination and state-supported accreditation, combine in a pincer movement to increase the vulnerability of service-class occupational groups.[8]

However, two important qualifications need to be made to this rather deterministic interpretation of the long-term effects of new technology on the service class. First, the trends that it reveals predate the invention and introduction of information technology. Second, the impact of technological change is extremely uneven in that some groups may be in a much better position to resist deskilling and rationalisation than others. As Ray[9] maintains, lower and middle-level managers have always been exposed to the various deskilling strategies initiated by top management from the early decades of the twentieth century onwards. From the very inception of their occupation in the early twentieth century, middle and – to a lesser extent – lower-level managers were technically deskilled and made responsible for securing the effective social organisation of shop-floor workers. Their skills and tasks were defined by higher-level management in such a way that they would remain in a subordinate position subject to the uncertainties and ambiguities of technological rationalisation and organisational control systems designed and evaluated by the former:

> Never, strictly speaking, possessing technical skill, losing large quantities of conceptual skill, managers have had no choice but to learn and deploy the social skills which others design based upon the assumptions about the human nature of workers. The acquisition of new social skills, however, does not give managers more power, autonomy or control over their own work process. Instead, the new skills merely keep them their jobs depending upon the adaptive capacity of individual managers, and their psychic capacity to cope successfully with constant ambiguity and uncertainty.[10]

The unevenness of the effects of new technology on service-class occupations relates both to variations in the speed and scale of implementation in different sectors of the economy[11] and to the differentially distributed capacities of various groups to resist and control technological innovations. Child suggests that three interrelated factors will determine the relative capacities of various groups within the service class to influence the direction and content of technological change in their favour: location in the workplace organisation, labour market situation and ideological function within the capitalist economic system:

> the more that white collar workers are strategically placed to be a party to decisions on new technology, the more likely they are to control its application in relation to their own jobs. . . . Secondly, the strength of white collar groups in the labour market is likely to have a general bearing on their ability to avoid heteronomy and a specific influence on the strength of their negotiating position over any proposals to introduce new technology. . . . Third . . . the ideological perspectives on the purpose of investment in information technology which are likely to prevail in public and private sectors respectively. The greater the weight that has been traditionally accorded to the quality of service in the public sector vis-à-vis considerations of cost is a factor likely to favour the maintenance by white-collar groups of their personal role in service provision against attempts to automate or technologically deskill on cost grounds.[12]

Thus, the ability of the medical profession to control technological innovation as compared to the inability of branch bank managers and officers to resist technologically induced deskilling and rationalisation can be accounted for in terms of the relative strength of the former in terms of its strategic organisational and institutional location; its maintenance of strong occupational associations exercising firm control over work and market situations with formal state support; and its preservation of an interdeterminate occupational knowledge-base in a direct relationship to the client reinforcing the legitimacy of an ideology of public service over that of cost reductions.

The relative ability of different occupational groups within the service class to resist work degradation and to control technological change will also depend upon the shifting priorities of employers in socio-technical reorganisation. As Elger suggests, there may be a general concern with 'cheapening and displacement of labour, diligence, flexibility, intensified work effort, and effective monitoring',[13] not to mention cost reductions in administrative and managerial overheads, but the extent to which these objectives will be strategically pursued during the introduction of new technology in particular sections of the economy may be open to question.

Recent evidence[14] suggests piecemeal and cumulative shifts in strategic initiatives undertaken by top-level management with considerable sectoral variations in the pattern of restructuring generated by technological innovation. Strategic offensives of an all-embracing character seem to be the exception rather than the rule, at least at the present time.

ORGANISATIONAL CHANGE

The contemporary drive for increased flexibility in working practices and work organisation emerged as one of the major themes of Chapter two.[15] The implications of this trend for the structure of management organisation and the character of managerial work now requires some assessment.

Streeck has argued that the search for flexibility has become something of a catch-all concept for everything and anything employers find desirable to increase operational efficiency and company profitability. He suggests, however, that employers' general pursuit of flexibility in production organisation may be defined in the following terms:

> Flexibility is sought as a property not just of industrial relations systems but of firms and production units as well. In this respect, it can be defined as a general capacity of enterprises to reorganize in close response to fluctuations in their environment. . . . Such flexibility is pursued both in the external and internal labour market. External flexibility consists basically of numerical flexibility which refers to the ease with which the numbers of workers employed can be adapted to meet fluctuations in demand. . . . Internal flexibility is in part 'functional flexibility' referring to the ease with which the tasks carried out by employees can be adapted to changes in demand. . . . Present demands of employers for more flexible systems of employment are inseparable from the simultaneous search of enterprises for higher flexibility of product ranges, technology, capital equipment, methods of finance, relationships with suppliers etc.[16]

Developments such as these are likely to have a significant impact on management structures and managerial work patterns. In particular, they will reinforce existing pressures for organisational rationalisation and increased cost-effectiveness, while simultaneously reducing opportunities and expectations over job security and career prospects for those managers excluded from the status of core, or central, workers within the enterprise. Thomas[17] has outlined a number of organisational changes associated with increased flexibility that are fundamentally calling into question the viability of the concept of career as a control device over managerial behaviour. These include decreasing expansion or absolute contraction in management structures and the career opportunities they provide; continuous demands for rationalisation and cost reductions in administrative and managerial overheads; reductions in job security, promotion prospects and employment status; minimal levels of intrinsic job satisfaction due to increased specialisation, routinisation and reduced task autonomy.

Taken together, Streeck's and Thomas's analyses seem to indicate that increasing numbers of managerial personnel – particularly those at the lower and middle reaches of the organisational hierarchy – are likely to find themselves excluded from internal, enterprise-based primary labour markets and the benefits – both material and symbolic – they provide (in terms of higher wages, better job security, improved welfare packages, more interesting and self-regulating work tasks, etc.). The status of lower- and middle-level managers as members of the employing organisation is minimised to a point where they become regarded as part of an external labour market that meets the changing needs of employers and top-level managers for numerical and functional flexibility in the face of strong turbulences and uncertainties in the political economies of advanced capitalist societies.

Not only is the viability of the notion of a managerial career as a control device called into question by these developments, but its significance as a crucial ideological support for a conception of managerial work as necessarily entailing notions of moral commitment and normative involvement is also radically undermined. As Anthony conveys the point:

> it seems very likely that we may be witnessing the destruction of the managerial ethos. It is destroyed as soon as the managers, who were recruited partly to apply it in the control of their subordinates, begin to see it applied to themselves. As

their work becomes more specialized, more intensively controlled or totally redundant they are forced to reject the assumptions and values which their recruitment and careers have taught them to adopt.[18]

Because pressures to achieve increased organisational flexibility generate polarisation within the managerial labour market between a relatively small élite of high-status service-class occupations and a much larger mass of proletarianised, routine white-collar workers subject to the insecurity and uncertainty of market-based employment systems, the long-term decline of a managerial work ideology embodying notions of trust and commitment seems inevitable. The problems of sustaining normative commitment and resisting a more instrumental attitude towards the job in the face of deep-seated socio-technical transformations that undermine the ideological foundations of managerial authority, seem too intractable for the service class to handle.

OCCUPATIONAL CHANGE

Research carried out on British management as an occupational group reveals very considerable diversity in social background, educational experiences, career profiles and work orientations. Mansfield, reviewing a series of occupational studies published between the mid-1950s and late 1970s, concluded that: 'In terms, therefore, of educational and social background any notion of "the average manager" is likely to be as lacking in utility as the concept of the "average man" '.[19] His review highlights the diverse social backgrounds of British managers, considerable variations in their career trajectories and employment conditions, and a wide range of affiliations to professional bodies and trade unions. It also suggests that very little had changed over the three decades covered by the various studies reviewed. While the total number of managers had increased, there was little sign of substantial change in the occupational character of management when set alongside dramatic changes in technology, economic conditions and social values. Indeed, Mansfield concludes with the thought that 'the considerable heterogeneity of managers may limit the extent to which the overall composition of the group has changed or will change in the future'.[20]

This picture of relatively 'static socio-economic heterogeneity' in the occupational composition of British management is largely confirmed in more recent studies by Poole, *et al.*,[21] Crockett and Elias,[22] and Snape and Bamber.[23] Poole, *et al.*, identify a situation of relative stability over time so that British management remains a highly differentiated occupational group in terms of social origins, educational backgrounds and career patterns. Recruitment to managerial positions was not an open process, but nor was it entirely closed in the sense that only 25 per cent of the total number of respondents surveyed originated in the professional and administrative category (that is, Category 1 of the Registrar General's occupational classification). The strategic interest groups impinging on the performance of the managerial task were considered to be owners and shareholders on the one hand, and consumers on the other. An ideological commitment to private enterprise remained very well entrenched, and state intervention in the economy was viewed with considerable suspicion – particularly by private sector managers.

Nevertheless, a number of developments occurring in the 1970s were thought to have weakened management's capacity to control corporate performance and to have generated a more instrumental attitude to work as the uncertainties and insecurities of economic life intensified. These included increased union power, moves in the direction of greater industrial democracy and socio-technical reorganisation at company and plant level reducing the contribution and status of operational managers.

Crockett and Elias confirm the relatively high degree of internal job mobility within management – particularly at the operational level:

> Managers are drawn mainly from the shop floor, that is, from supervisory, craft and operative occupations. We find that managerial jobs are not highly stable occupations in the sense that once one becomes a manager, one stays a manager. A considerable number of managers moved out of a managerial occupation held in 1965 into a professional occupation. Most surprisingly, we found that, of those persons who were managers in 1965, but were no longer classified into a managerial position in 1975–76, 17 per cent had moved into an operative occupation. Much greater occupational stability was found in professional, scientific and qualified engineering occupations.[24]

However, Snape and Bamber[25] suggest that the proportion of managers starting their working lives in manual or clerical jobs was declining as the significance of formal educational credentials – both for initial entry and subsequent upward mobility – was increasing. Yet, they maintain that management is not a closed social élite in that the relative dominance of middle-class family backgrounds in initial recruitment and subsequent mobility is balanced by continuing substantial entry from clerical and manual categories – at least to the lower and middle ranks of the occupational hierarchy within management. Legatt provides a useful summary of the overall conclusions to be drawn from these occupational studies:

> Managers, as a group, were found to be neither homogeneous nor in their principal characteristics changing over time . . . managers can be seen to be a differentiated group and to reflect the relationships in the wider society that are essentially shaped by the existing class structure.[26]

Goldthorpe's research on initial recruitment into and subsequent mobility within higher-level service-class positions also reflects a relatively fluid situation within an overall pattern of comparative stability:

> the pressure of demand for professional, administrative and managerial employees, at least over the period since the Second World War, has meant that the basis for recruitment to the service class has been very wide. Results from national studies of social mobility regularly indicate that only a minority – usually between a quarter and a third – of men (and women) presently found in service class positions are in fact the offspring of parents who held such positions . . . while national mobility studies regularly reveal a wide basis of inter-generational recruitment to service class positions, they also reveal, with no less regularity, that expanding service classes preserve a high degree of inter-generational stability. . . . Not only, then, do individuals, once established in the service class, tend to retain their positions, but a similar tendency may be said to apply in the case of their families also; and the demographic identity of the service class, is of course, in this way further developed.[27]

This leads Goldthorpe to conclude that the service class has the capacity to secure its own reproduction in terms of its continuing expansion and consolidation. It also provides further support for a widening split within management between lower-level supervisory and clerical workers, who are increasingly detached from their higher-level counterparts in administrative, professional and managerial positions. Thus, the service class seems to be in a position to control the mechanisms whereby recruitment into its ranks, and the advantages this bestows in terms of superior life chances of both an economic and cultural kind, is secured against excessive penetration by lower-class groupings. At the same time, this control – particularly over the process whereby individuals become 'credentialled' for entry into higher-level positions – is potentially threatened by the technological, organisational and political changes documented in this and previous chapters.

As Scott[28] and others[29] have shown, the service class is very far from securing the degree of social closure and class reproduction enjoyed by the owning class in terms of the latter's strong control over recruitment mechanisms and the cohesiveness of its internal social integration. Indeed, Goldthorpe may be correct when he points to the lack of any firm evidence for predicting the decomposition of the service class and its eventual decline as a socio-political force. Previous discussion, however, suggests that it does remain vulnerable to the longer-term impact of technological and organisational change directed towards increased rationalisation and centralisation. While the immediate effects of these changes may be limited to the lower and middle ranks of the managerial hierarchy at the moment, we should not underestimate their potential to spread to higher-level postions. This is particularly true when we remember the severe limitations placed upon the capacity of the service class to engage in co-ordinated social action as a collective agent defending the institutional and ideological foundations of its superior life chances.[30]

Previous discussion indicates that longer-term changes taking place in the technological, organisational, occupational and political environment in which management is located may pose a serious threat to its continued authority and status, as well as to the economic and cultural advantages derived from its strategic position within the division of labour. The various options open to managers in this increasingly threatening environment are reviewed in the following sections. Three possible options will be assessed in relation to the potential they offer for mounting an effective managerial response to the challenges posed by structural changes to the political economies of advanced capitalist societies.

PROFESSIONALISATION

As a strategy of social closure – that is, as a set of interrelated processes and mechanisms for mobilising power in defence of collective control over a group's share of rewards or resources – professionalisation may have much to recommend itself to modern-day managers. As a form of collective action designed to maximise claims to rewards and opportunities by denying entry to actual or potential competition – that is, by excluding the latter from occupations of privileged positions within the stratification system – professionalisation has been spectacularly successful for certain groups such as doctors, lawyers and architects. As Parkin remarks:

> Professionalization itself may be understood as a strategy designed, amongst other things, to limit and control the supply of entrants to an occupation in order to safeguard or enhance its market value . . . credentialism stands out as a doubly effective device for protecting the learned professions from the hazards of the market place. Not merely does it serve the convenient purpose of monitoring and restricting the supply of labour, but also effectively masks all but the most extreme variations in the level of ability of professional members.[31]

Indeed, there is some evidence to suggest that British management has been infused by notions of professional identity and status throughout its historical development from the latter decades of the nineteenth century onwards. Child, *et al.* describe this process in these terms:

> Notions of professionalism have infused British management in two ways, which paradoxically appear to carry contradictory implications. There has been much debate from the earliest days of the management movement on the question of professionalism. At the same time, there is a long history among specialist functions attached to management, and

claiming to form part of it, of nurturing collective associations promoting professionalism among members of the speciality. This professionalism *within* management tends to foster a distinct identity among specialists, controlling entry through special examination requirements and occupational qualifications. The idea of *management* as a profession is a unitary concept, while the idea of professionalism within management has fragmentary implications.[32]

Contradiction and consequent fragmentation within the ideology of professional management have reinforced the structural obstacles that stand in the way of achieving the central precondition for a successful strategy of social closure based on professionalisation – that is, gaining and retaining monopoly control over indeterminate forms of knowledge and practice that cannot easily be appropriated by others.

Three major obstacles stand in the way of managers realising a successful strategy of social closure based on professionalism. First, the existing patterns of professionalisation within management has encouraged competition and conflict between different hierarchical levels and specialist functions aimed at enhancing the contribution which they make – or at least are seen to make – to the long-term objective of capital accumulation and denying the actual or potential contribution of other organisational professions.[33] The consequent internal fragmentation has made it extremely difficult for managers to construct and maintain a viable professional occupational identity that would gain ideological acceptance and support from society in general and the state in particular. Lack of state support for a strategy of closure through professionalisation may be a serious weakness, particularly when we remember the historical significance of the former for the legitimisation of the established or traditional professions. Thus, Johnson argues:

> that both the emergent forms of the liberal-bourgeois state and the later construction of an imperial state apparatus involved the transformation of professional occupations as processes integral to that of state formation. . . . The developing relationship of professions to state helped to define the limits and potentialities of state powers, functions and capacities, as well as conditioning the possibility of independent action by occupational colleague networks. . . . Profes-

sionalization, where it occurs, is indicative of a particular form of articulation between the state and those occupations which have been of particular significance in the state's historical formation.[34]

Second, the organisational dependence of managers creates severe institutional difficulties for the successful implementation of professionalisation. Their dependence on large-scale bureaucratic organisations for employment, remuneration, authority and status exposes them to processes of rationalisation that drastically limit and reduce the degree of self-managed autonomy and expertise conventionally associated with traditional professional groups. As Child[35] suggests, the extent to which 'corporate professionals' such as accountants, engineers and scientists may be subjected to a process of proletarianisation – that is, the imposition of bureaucratic controls that lead to systematic deskilling and labour-market deterioration – may have been substantially overestimated by a number of commentators. However, there is some evidence to suggest that:

> To the extent that organizational incentives and controls and the bureaucratic ethos of loyalty prevail, the wider professional community from which individual orientations derived some sustenance will be splintered. This outcome is very likely in the case of experts in the managerial and executive roles . . . dominant interests will use whatever means seem practical in order to domesticate the body of managers and executives and turn it into a pliant instrument of their goals.[36]

Third, the character of the existing knowledge-base available to managers presents formidable problems for closure through professionalisation. While the established professions have been able to assert and defend the indeterminate or tacit status of their occupational knowledge – that is, its resistance to explicit and systematic testing that would render it in a form appropriate to standardisation and formalisation of a procedural or rule-bound kind – the newer professions have found this objective much more difficult to achieve. Insofar as the established professions have achieved this strategic goal, then they are in a position to assert that their practice cannot be subjected to external monitoring and control because of its indeterminate and judgemental quality. Not only is managerial practice evidently exposed to such externally imposed control processes, but managers themselves are mainly employed to design and monitor the systems through which effective surveillance may be realised. This leads Clegg, *et al.*, to conclude, that the 'organizational professions, which are said to be the major constitutional element of the new middle class, are themselves part of an increasingly routinised division of labour which penetrates the profession and provides the framework for class divisions within the professional occupations themselves'.[37]

Consequently, a strategy of social closure based on full professionalisation would seem extremely difficult, if not impossible, for management to achieve. However, partial professionalisation – particularly for those in élite service-class positions within corporate hierarchies – would seem to be a more realistic basis on which to defend and enhance occupational power and control. This is likely to reinforce existing pressures towards polarisation between a professional salaried middle class and a proletarianised routine white-collar class. Yet, it may provide a coherent and viable strategy of social closure through which the managerial élite or service class could effectively defend itself against the threats outlined in previous discussion.

UNIONISATION

A second possible response to the challenges described in previous sections is that of unionisation. The logic of previous analysis would suggest that this collective response is likely to be most prominent within the ranks of lower and middle-level management, given their relatively high degree of exposure to what Fox has characterised as the 'low trust dynamic' at work in advanced capitalist societies:

> collective action may reach further up in the management ranks than was earlier expected. A number of factors now discernable may promote among middle managers a growing consciousness that individual action is no longer enough to ensure their own welfare – growth in company size; increasing application to themselves of bureaucratic rules; the speed of performance–measurement techniques and appraisal methods which sow the seeds of a feeling that they are being

watched and no longer fully trusted; the threats to their security presented by takeovers, rationalization, and office automation. Out of this consciousness seems likely to develop the pursuit of some degree of collective security by imposing discretion-reducing rules or understandings upon top management.[38]

Simpson[39] has extended this analysis and identifies five major areas of change that are likely to increase pressure on lower and middle-level managers: reduced pay differentials, constraining labour legislation, the challenge of workplace trade unionism, organisational rationalisation and worker-participation schemes. While Simpson accepts that the impact of these changes is likely to be very uneven,[40] he suggests that they may provide a set of conditions in which trade union organisation and action looks more attractive as a defence against further encroachments upon managerial authority and discretion. This may be particularly true in situations where a potent combination of senior management disinterest and neglect, intensified organisational and technological rationalisation, and a growing instrumentalism in work orientations brought about by much reduced levels of job satisfaction push increasing numbers of lower and middle managers into union membership. Denied any realistic hope of defence and enhancement through professionalisation, an increasing proportion of lower and middle-level managers may turn to trade unionism as a resource offering some chance of collective protection and improvement in a hostile environment.

Empirical research[41] on managerial trade unionism indicates that the push of the 'low trust dynamic' highlighted by Fox and Simpson may encourage a more positive attitude to collective organisation and representation among lower and middle-level managers. However, it also suggests that the form of trade unionism in which managers are likely to engage will be substantially different – particularly in ideological and operational terms – from that associated with traditional unionism.

Armstrong argues that the major motivation for advocating some means of collective organisation and representation for lower and middle management is the objective of regaining 'a greater share in decision making within the function of capital'.[42] He develops this argument in the following terms:

there are four strands of evidence consistent with the view that white collar unionization contains, as a potential issue, the restoration of the lost influence and autonomy of supervisors within the control function of capital. These are (i) that actual or potential managerial trade unionists are concerned to pursue this issue, via collective means, (ii) that for supervisors, unionization may be a question of collective mobilization against the power of shop floor unions, (iii) that the demand for unionization amongst managers and supervisors is essentially a demand for *separate* representation, (iv) that the economic concerns behind white collar unionization are a concern to restore a *differential* in relation to manual workers as a whole and that this may be seen as the first reward for discharging the control functions of capital as well as for knowledge or specialized skills.[43]

This leads him to conclude that managerial unionism is a means of ensuring collective mobilisation and representation of sectional interests within capitalist control structures deemed to be neglected by and underrepresented within senior management élites. This is borne out, for example, in Child and Partridge's research, which shows that a deteriorating internal labour market position and increased proximity to manual workers attaining readily observable benefits from unionism had encouraged the development of a much more positive attitude to union membership on the part of supervisors. However, this was not viewed as in any way undermining a continued normative commitment to and identification with the employing organisation:

> The rationale which most of the supervisors had about belonging to a union is not of the traditional proletarian type based upon an identification with a lower and socially exploited class of shop floor workers. They generally saw no incompatibility between a commitment to union membership and identification with management. The strongest point of identification was, however, with their own middle manager supervisors rather than with senior management, alias 'the company'.[44]

Weir's[45] research on a large group of middle managers' perceptions of trade union organisation and collective bargaining within a big, profitable company in the food and drink industry shows that unionism was favoured as a means of improving the effectiveness of the formal consultative machinery through which their interests could be represented. Rather than viewing managerial unionism either as an expression of growing white collar dissent or as an indirect mechanism for increasing employer control, most middle managers included in this survey viewed the former as a means for more adequately representing their own functional interests within a generally collaborative relationship with the employer.

An increasing propensity to join trade unions among lower and middle-level managers – particularly among those located in the public sector[46] – is evident in recent empirical research. The latter also suggests that unionisation is usually seen as a strategy for defending collective interests that are deemed to be threatened by encroaching rationalisation, continued senior management apathy, and developments in workplace blue-collar trade unionism that have further reduced managerial autonomy at lower levels. However, the form of unionism this strategy generates is likely to be very different to that of conventional blue-collar trade unionism. While managerial trade unions represent the interests of their members in areas such as collective bargaining, grievance and disputes procedures, and conflict-regulation processes, their ideological profile and *modus operandi* sets them apart from blue-collar unions. Carter contends that the quite rapid unionisation of supervisors and managers that took place in the 1970s – many of them affiliated to the Trades Union Congress – :

> does not represent a positive break with previous thought nor does it indicate a new identification with the labour movement. It is merely a more effective way of pressing managers' interests which are still seen as being quite distinct from, and in opposition to, those of manual workers . . . not only do the majority of managers not have economic ownership of the means of production, but they also have diminishing powers over day-to-day decisions and their own conditions of work. These changing circumstances necessitated the putting aside of ideological objections to TUC-affiliated unions in order for managers to press their interests more effectively. With the weakening of trade union power and confidence, and the prospect of a Conservative government increasingly hostile to trade union organization, a simple evolutionary path towards

greater managerial unionization seems unlikely.[47]

In this respect, unionisation among lower and middle-level managers may be interpreted as an attempt to restore a deteriorating labour market position and regain eroded control functions within the labour process, without in any way threatening continued ideological identification with the aims and values of top-level management and private owners.

PRIVATISATION

Both of the responses available to, and utilised by, managers, which have been discussed so far, require collective behaviour of some kind or another. However, as Simpson[48] notes, a third option is available, which takes a much more individualistic form – that is, the retreat into private life and radically reduced job commitments undertaken by individual managers as the only sensible response to growing personal dissatisfaction with the state of their current work situations. An increasing propensity towards instrumentalism and minimal job performance is seen to dovetail with a rejection of an alienating work environment that cannot be improved through collective action, but only avoided through individual withdrawal into non-work activities.

How extensive this response is, or is likely to become, among managerial personnel is very difficult, if not impossible, to determine at the present time. Kay's[49] research on individual coping strategies among American middle managers suggests that increasing numbers are choosing either complete exit or minimal performance coupled with privatisation as viable responses to the meaningless character of their work situations. Research[50] on levels of physiological and psychological stress among managers has identified a number of factors that may be contributing to a situation in which increased pressure and tension on individuals is not being sufficiently recognised or responded to in the appropriate manner. In particular, increases in job workload and intensified role ambiguity and conflict[51] generated by organisational restructuring have been seen to exacerbate the problem of managerial stress and the personal withdrawal from work that it often engenders.

Consequently, the phenomenon of the 'unemployed self', which

Gouldner[52] so eloquently described as a feature of employed work in modern industrial society, may become a more prominent feature of managerial employment in the future. The industrial system, Gouldner argues:

> rewards and fosters those skills deemed useful and suppresses the expression of talents and faculties deemed useless, and thereby structures and imprints itself upon the individual personality and self. . . . In short, vast parts of any personality must be suppressed or repressed in the course of playing a role in industrial society. . . . Thus, just as there are unemployed men, there is also the unemployed self. Here, then, in the exclusions of self fostered by an industrial system oriented towards utility, is a fundamental source of the sense of a life wasted which is so pervasive, even if muffled, in an industrial society. For the excluded self, while muffled, is not voiceless and makes its protest heard.[53]

While this protest is likely to take a variety of forms, one response that may assume increasing salience within management is to reject the idea that managerial work will provide – or ought to provide – a source of personal satisfaction and meaning. Instead, managers may be forced to search for these qualities in non-work settings where the unemployed self can be reclaimed and redeemed.

THE END OF MANAGEMENT

The scale of the threat posed to conventional managerial structures and ideologies by the long-term changes outlined in this chapter, and the weakness of the response it has elicited from managers, has led some commentators to predict the end of management as we have come to know it in western industrial societies. Not only are managers seen as failing to provide a viable defence of conventional structures and ideologies, but they are also contributing to their own demise insofar as they are developing systems and controls that will lead to the redundancy of many of the functions they currently perform.[54]

Thus, Fletcher maintains that:

> 'manager' will cease to be a category of employee in the

foreseeable future. . . . Within a company the intricate and delicate management structure will disappear and be replaced by a managerial atmosphere in which highly paid experts execute precise control, observation, and distraction tasks for their masters using machines which also control themselves. By attrition, redundancy, unionization or revolution management will be finished, and managers themselves are facilitating their own end.[55]

Similar prognoses are made by Anthony[56] and Pym.[57] Anthony argues that the destruction of the ideology of managerial work is paralleled by the demise of managerial organisation brought about by increasing rationalisation and redundancy. Consequently, 'the crippled monstrosities which were produced by the division of labour now seem to have their counterparts in the managerial sector, for they seem to be crippled to the extent that they have been made unemployable by the very forces that produced them'.[58] Pym suggests that the increasing size and complexity of work organisations has produced interdependent control systems that shift authority and responsibility from the individual manager to the collective concern. As a result, 'the manager in the medium-sized to large concern is finding great difficulty in deriving a sense of achievement from his tasks'.[59] The typical managerial response is to deny that this crisis in institutional role and identity exists. Instead, a massive arsenal of symbols, meetings, games and systems are invented 'which provide the delusions of purpose, tangibility, personal responsibility and performance'.[60]

Each of these commentators is conveying the general argument that current managerial thinking and action is trapped within an ideological frame of reference and an institutional framework that hold an increasingly tenuous relationship to the real world that late-twentieth-century managers inhabit. Entrapped within a work ideology that is continually undermined by socio-technical change and an institutional framework that is ill-equipped to respond to the pressure for continual rationalisation and the tensions this creates, modern management is unable to fashion a response to the major challenges of our time that holds any moral authority or practical effectiveness.

However, both Pym and Anthony are prepared to offer advice as to how this situation may be improved and eventual managerial extinction possibly avoided. The former argues that the manager's dependence on 'linear, sequential, symmetrical thinking' and bureaucratised employment systems is the ultimate cause of the problem. Bureaucratic thinking and administration produce employment systems that are strong on specialisation and standardisation, but weak when it comes to integrating the 'personal and social chaos born of over-differentiation'. Only a frontal attack on the coercive institutions of employment in industrial societies will release managers from their subordination to, and dependence upon, bureaucratic structures:

> We require a gradual disengagement from these tyrannical conditions. . . . Initially employers and employees having collectively recognized the poverty of their lives would need to determine those classes of employee best suited to alternative conditions and match this with the people prepared to be guinea pigs on some trial basis. Undoubtedly such an experiment would apply best to those who do least work, men and women in service functions, managers, professionals, technicians and clerks in particular. Though this suggestion has the appearance of yet another soft option for the ruling classes in fact it would be anything but easy for men and women still clinging to the last vestiges of the Protestant ethic. . . . Renegotiated conditions of employment would aid those related causes of freedom, meaning, reality and understanding through the freeing up of time and space.[61]

Anthony looks to educational reform and the reconstruction of an employment strategy based on the moral foundations provided by traditional – as opposed to sophisticated – paternalism as potential sources of salvation. He argues that any educational process that persuaded managers to accept their moral responsibility for creating and sustaining human communities engaged in co-operative effort founded upon mutual trust and reciprocity would secure a moral base for managerial authority 'in a concern for the integrity and good of the community that it governs'.[62]

Yet, the formidable ideological and institutional – not to mention material – constraints within which any radical transformation in managerial thinking and conduct has to be attempted are clearly recognised by both authors. Indeed, the accumulated weight of the evidence reviewed in this and previous chapters implies that contemporary conditions are unlikely to facilitate moves in the directions required by Pym and Anthony. The pressures towards more centralised, instrumentally based forms of work organisation and control, in which utilitarian considerations and priorities are the overriding demand that management must meet, seem to be irresistible. Nevertheless, previous discussion has also suggested that these pressures can be, and have been, resisted and turned to good effect in the past. Whether managers are able or willing to overcome the obstacles that stand in the way of constructing a more meaningful and satisfactory work environment for themselves and others remains to be seen. This time it may be their own existence that is at stake.

REFERENCES

1. Wood, S. (ed.), *The Degradation of Work?* (Hutchinson, London, 1982).
2. Gill, C., *Work, Unemployment and the New Technology* (Polity Press, Cambridge, 1985).
3. Kay, E., *The Crisis in Middle Management* (American Management Asociation, New York, 1974); Child, J., Loveridge, R.; Harvey, J. and Spencer, A., 'Microelectronics and the Quality of Employment in Services', in Marstrand, P. (ed.), *New Technology and the Future of Work and Skills* (Francis Pinter, London, 1987).
4. Child, J., 'New Technology and the Service Class', in Purcell, K., Wood, S., Waton, A. and Allen, S. (eds.), *The Changing Experience of Employment* (Macmillan, London, 1987).
5. Gill, op. cit., (1985), pp. 104–5.
6. Child, J., *Organization: A Guide to Problems and Practice* (Harper and Row, London, 2nd edition, 1984), p. 261.
7. Child, op. cit., (1987), p. 132.
8. Child, *et al.*, op. cit., (1987).
9. Ray, C.A., 'The Conceptual Deskilling and Social Reskilling of Line Managers', Unpublished Paper, Sociology Board, Merrill College, University of California, 1985.
10. Ibid., p. 31.
11. On this point see Gill, op. cit., (1985), and Elger, A., 'Flexible Futures?: New Technology and the Contemporary Transformation of Work' in *Work, Employment and Society*, vol. 1, (1984), pp. 528–40.
12. Child, op. cit., (1984), p. 150. 'Heteronomy' refers to strategies aimed at incorporating professional groups within standardised administrative routines and systems.
13. Elger, op. cit., (1987), p. 533.
14. Daniel, W.W., *Workplace Industrial Relations and Technical Change* (Francis Pinter, London, 1984).

15. For recent empirical evidence on the drive for flexibility in manufacturing operations see Edwards, P.K., *Factory Managers* (Basil Blackwell, Oxford, 1987).

16. Streeck, W., 'The Uncertainties of Management in the Management of Uncertainty: Employers, Labour Relations and Industrial Adjustment in the 1980s,' *Work, Employment and Society*, vol. 1, (1984), pp. 281–308.

17. Thomas, A., 'Managerial Careers and the Problem of Control', Paper to European Group on Organization Studies *Conference on Capital and Control*, University of York, 1981.

18. Anthony, P.D., *The Ideology of Work* (Tavistock, London, 1977), p. 297.

19. Mansfield, R., 'Who are the Managers?', in Poole, M. and Mansfield, R. (eds.), *Managerial Roles in Industrial Relations* (Gower, Aldershot, 1980), pp. 12–20.

20. Ibid., p. 20.

21. Poole, M., Mansfield, R., Blyton, P. and Frost, P., *Managers in Focus: The British Manager in the Early 1980s* (Gower, Aldershot, 1981).

22. Crockett, G. and Elias, P., 'British Managers: A Study of their Education, Training, Mobility and Earnings', *British Journal of Industrial Relations*, vol. 22, (1984), pp. 34–46.

23. Snape, E.J. and Bamber, G.J., *Managerial and Professional Employees in Britain*, Employee Relations, vol. 9, (1987).

24. Crockett and Elias, op. cit., (1984). However, Crockett and Elias proceed on the basis of a relatively narrow operational definition of manager insofar as they exclude professional and technical staff.

25. Snape and Bamber, op. cit., (1987).

26. Legatt, T., 'Managers in Industry: Their Background and Education', *Sociological Review*, vol. 26, (1978), pp. 807–25.

27. Goldthorpe, J., 'On the Service Class', in Giddens, A. and Mackenzie, G. (eds.), *Social Class and the Division of Labour* (Cambridge University Press, Cambridge, 1982), pp. 162–85 (pp. 172–7).

28. Scott, J., *Corporations, Classes and Capitalism* (Hutchinson, London, 2nd edition, 1985).

29. Stanworth, P. and Giddens, A. (eds.), *Elites and Power in British Society* (Cambridge University Press, Cambridge, 1974).

30. This point has already been discussed at greater length in Chapter five.

31. Parkin, F., *Marxism and Class Theory: A Bourgeois Critique* (Tavistock, London, 1979), pp. 54–6.

32. Child, J., Fores, M., Glover, I. and Lawrence, P., 'A Price to Pay?: Professionalism and Work Organization in Britain and West Germany', *Sociology*, vol. 17, (1983), pp. 63–78 (p. 67). For a critique of the argument these commentators present see McCormick, K.J., 'Professionalism and Work Organizations: Some Loose Ends and Open Questions', *Sociology*, vol. 19, (1985), pp. 285–94.

33. Armstrong, P., 'Competition Between the Organizational Professions and the Evolution of Management Control Strategies', in Thompson, K. (ed.), *Work, Employment and Unemployment* (Open University

Press, Milton Keynes, 1984), pp. 97–120.

34. Johnson, T. 'The State and the Professions: Peculiarities of the British', in Giddens and Mackenzie (eds.), op. cit., (1982), pp. 186–208.

35. Child, J., 'Professionals in the Corporate World: Values, Interests and Control', in Dunkerley, D. and Salaman, G. (eds.), *The International Yearbook of Organization Studies* (Routledge and Kegan Paul, London, 1982), pp. 212–41.

36. Rueschemeyer, D., *Power and the Division of Labour* (Polity Press, Cambridge, 1986), pp. 134–5.

37. Clegg, S., Boreham, P. and Dow, G., *Class, Politics and the Economy* (Routledge and Kegan Paul, London, 1986), p. 192. The extent to which notions of professionalism provide an ideological resource to be drawn upon by protagonists in the current debate about the future of management education and training is revealed in three recently published reports that are highly critical of the amateurish quality of British provision when compared to our major international competitors. On this point, see Mangham, I.L. and Silver, M.S., *Management Training: Context and Practice* (School of Management, University of Bath, 1986); Constable, J. and McCormick, R., *The Making of British Managers* (British Institute of Management, London, 1987); Handy, C., *The Making of Managers* (National Economic Development Office, London, 1987). For a longer-term perspective on the debate over the contribution education and training should make to the professionalisation of British managers, see Whitley, R., Thomas, A. and Marceau, J., *Masters of Business?: Business Schools and Business Graduates in Britain and France* (Tavistock, London, 1981). The latter study suggests that internal differentiation within the managerial labour force as a whole, combined with the cultural rather than technical criteria that are the predominant considerations informing recruitment decisions made by controllers of the élite managerial labour market, will place severe limitations on any substantial moves towards greater professionalisation through educational credentialism.

38. Fox, A., *Beyond Contract: Work, Power and Trust Relations* (Faber and Faber, London, 1974), p. 328.

39. Simpson, D., 'The Industrial Relations of Managers', in Poole and Mansfield, op. cit., (1980), pp. 102–15.

40. Many of the constraints placed upon the exercise of managerial prerogative highlighted by Simpson have been considerably eased in the 1980s – for instance, the radical transformation of the labour-legislation environment in which management now operates.

41. Weir, D., 'Radical Managerialism: Middle Managers' Perceptions of Collective Bargaining', *British Journal of Industrial Relations*, vol. 14, (1976), pp. 324–38; Poole, M., Mansfield, R., Blyton, P. and Frost, P., 'Why Managers Join Unions: Evidence from Britain', *Industrial Relations*, vol. 22, (1983), pp. 426–44; Child, J. and Partridge, B., *Lost Managers: Supervisors in Industry and Society* (Cambridge University Press, Cambridge, 1982); Simpson, D., 'Managers in Workers' Trade

Unions: The Case of the National Union of Journalists', in Thurley, K. and Wood, S. (eds.), *Industrial Relations and Management Strategy* (Cambridge University Press, Cambridge, 1983), pp. 19–26; Bamber, G., *Militant Managers?: Managerial Unionism and Industrial Relations* (Gower, Aldershot, 1986); Armstrong, P., Carter, B., Smith, C. and Nichols, T., *White Collar Workers, Trade Unions and Class* (Croom Helm, London, 1986).

42. Armstrong, P., 'Work Supervisors and Trade Unionism', in Armstrong, P., *et al.*, op. cit., (1986), p. 110.
43. Ibid., p. 121.
44. Child and Partridge, op. cit., (1982), p. 188.
45. Weir, op. cit., (1976).
46. Poole, *et al.*, op. cit., (1981), calculated that 25 per cent of British managers were union members at the time of their study. There is a marked contrast, however, between public and private sector representation – 60 per cent of public-sector managers were members of unions of some sort or another, but only 9 per cent of private-sector managers were in unions. A key factor here is obviously the much higher levels of state encouragement and employer support for managerial unionisation in the public sector.
47. Carter, B., *Capitalism, Class Conflict and the New Middle Class* (Routledge and Kegan Paul, London, 1985), pp. 201–2.
48. Simpson, op. cit., (1980).
49. Kay, op. cit., (1974).
50. Cooper, C.L., 'Sources of Stress on Managers at Work', in Cooper, C.L. (ed.), *Psychology and Management* (Macmillan, London, 1981), pp. 201–21.
51. Role ambiguity refers to a situation in which there is a lack of adequate information and definitional clarity about the work objectives associated with a particular work role. Role conflict refers to a situation in which there are conflicting job demands integral to the same work role.
52. Gouldner, A., 'The Unemployed Self', in Fraser, R. (ed.), *Work: Twenty Personal Accounts*, vol. 2 (Penguin, Harmondsworth, 1969), pp. 346–65.
53. Ibid., pp. 348–9.
54. Child, op. cit., (1987).
55. Fletcher, C., 'The End of Management', in Child, J. (ed.), *Man and Organization* (Allen and Unwin, London, 1973), pp. 135–57.
56. Anthony, op. cit., (1977).
57. Pym, D., 'The Demise of Management and the Ritual of Unemployment', *Human Relations*, vol. 26, (1973), pp. 675–88.
58. Anthony, op. cit., (1977), p. 297.
59. Pym, op. cit., (1973), p. 683.
60. Ibid., p. 683.
61. Ibid., p. 693–4.
62. Anthony, P.D., *The Foundations of Management* (Tavistock, London, 1986), p. 198.

7

CONCLUSION

In certain respects, sociological research and analysis have tended to reinforce, rather than question, the stereotypical image of management as a rational process geared to the achievement of instrumental goals through the deployment of an efficient organisational technology.

The general thrust of the argument developed in this book has been aimed at undermining that stereotype and revealing its severe limitations. The exposition and assessment of material relating to each of the substantive themes providing the overall framework for this book has consistently displayed the inherent weaknesses of a technocratic reading of management. The latter conveys an image of management as a neutral – or neutered – body of functionaries concerned only with the design, construction and evaluation of an organisational technology that will provide the most effective and efficient means of co-ordinating and controlling work behaviour.

The intellectual poverty and practical impotence of this interpretation has been repeatedly exposed throughout this book. The influence it continues to exert on even the most radical or advanced forms of thinking and analysis should not be underestimated. Its pervasive hold on exponents of theoretical perspectives, which are assumed to have broken with functionalism and systems theory, needs to be resisted. In particular, its treatment of management as an inert identity that is programmed by external forces of one sort or another that are totally beyond its influence, much less control, must be rejected.

This can be achieved only through the development of alternative perspectives that approach management as a set of diverse and loosely interrelated social practices concerned with assembling and controlling the dispersed pattern of social relations through which work is performed and reviewed. This set of practices will necessarily embody a rich mixture of moral, political, cultural and technical ingredients. The ways in which these ingredients interact and the consequences that flow from such interaction are usually unpredictable and often unforeseen. This merely reflects the complex and contradictory nature of that set of activities and relations that are constituted through the practice of management. While the latter is performed within a framework of structural and ideological constraints that cannot be simply wished away, they actually provide the context in which managerial practice is engaged – a context which is itself partially redefined and reworked through the efforts of managers.

Considered in this way, the sociology of management can be seen to continue that traditional concern with the 'problematic of human agency' which Dawe[1] argues is central to any understanding of the history of sociological thought and analysis. Dawe's interpretation of the latter suggests that the concept of social action has provided a medium through which the inherently ambiguous and contradictory nature of human agency can be expressed. In particular, it has served as a focal point for a dialogue stretching over several centuries, which has revealed the 'dismal paradox that human agency becomes human bondage because of the very nature of human agency'.[2] By facilitating a debate over the social processes whereby 'action succumbs to powers and constraints which are themselves the products of action',[3] Dawe believes that sociology has illuminated, if not overcome, the fundamental dilemma of the human condition as simultaneously embodying the most creative and destructive aspects of social life.

The ambiguous and paradoxical character of human agency is clearly reflected in the contribution that sociology has made to our understanding of management. At one and the same time management reflects the drive towards instrumental rationality as an inherent characteristic of human agency and stands testimony to the inability of human beings to realise it in anything like its ideal form. Cursed with the burden of creating order out of chaos, managers find themselves in a situation where the need to achieve control through organisation requires engagement in practices that inevitably negate the very instrumental objectives to which they are officially directed. Schooled in the rhetoric of theories and techniques that are supposed to guarantee an acceptable degree of calculated order and control, managers face a social reality that demands moral and political relationships that continually undermine the logic of instrumental rationality. The drive to dominate and control social life through the elaboration and extension of organisational systems generates consequences and responses that undermine the very rationale in which these objectives take on general meaning and significance.

Insofar as it has improved our understanding of the social reality of which managers are a crucial part, then sociology has made a useful, perhaps vital, contribution to our appreciation of the unavoidable ambiguities and predicaments that we all face. It may also provide some assistance in developing forms of analysis and conduct through which greater insight and sensitivity can be displayed when undertaking those social practices through which we attempt to manage an environment that we all share.

REFERENCES

1. Dawe, A., 'Theories of Social Action', in Bottomore, T. and Nisbet, R. (eds.), *A History of Sociological Analysis* (Heinemann, London, 1979), pp. 362–417. The significance of the 'paradox of human agency' for an understanding of the development of organisational analysis as a field of study is explored in Reed, M., 'The Problem of Human Agency in Organizational Analysis', *Organization Studies*, vol. 9, No. 1, (January 1988).
2. Ibid., p. 398.
3. Abrams, P., *Historical Sociology* (Open Books, Somerset, 1982), p. xiv.

INDEX